Paul Tautges and Eric Kress have given to us a wonderful exposition of the often neglected book of Lamentations. Not only have they brought the full meaning of the text to the surface, but they have filled the commentary with practical suggestions of ways in which this much needed teaching on how to act in the midst of deep suffering can be carried out to the glory of God and the personal enrichment of each individual believer. I heartily recommend this book for those who are in times of deep distress and for the body of Christ that needs to be prepared for every possible form of suffering that may come our way, or that may come in the lives of those we need to reach out to for the glory of God.

—Walter C. Kaiser, Jr.
President Emeritus
Gordon-Conwell Theological Seminary

Books by Bible teachers that combine solid exposition, theological depth, and pastoral wisdom are very rare. They might include one of these strengths, seldom two, but almost never all three. This book on Lamentations, however, is just such a book! It is a tremendous accomplishment. It is at one and the same time a verse-by-verse commentary, a rich devotional treasury, and a very capable biblical counselor's guide. I cannot say enough good things about it. Seasoned shepherds, Eric Kress and Paul Tautges are uniquely qualified to write on this somewhat unfamiliar Old Testament book. They combine the skill of preachers, the acumen of theologians, and the sensitivity of counselors. For both pastors and laymen alike, this book fills a great need. I am grateful for this addition to the Kress Biblical Resources line of volumes. It will surely do its part to edify the church of Jesus Christ.

—Lance Quinn
Pastor-Teacher
Bethany Church on the Hill

Rarely is a divinely inspired work, especially when endowed with such beautifully crafted poetry, so routinely ignored by Christians. Yet that is the lot of this work by Jeremiah. Employing a combination of acrostics and unusual meter, this "weeping prophet" intricately intersperses his despair and lament with astonishing songs of solace and thanksgiving. Fortunately, authors Kress and Tautges have brought this small prophecy to life for us, pulling it out of the shadows of neglect and drawing us irresistibly to its timeless lessons. Plumbing the depths of the prophets is not always simple, yet these authors, with their distinctively pastoral style, make it easy to access the truths of this prophecy and apply its eternal principles. And in doing so, they have remarkably captured both depth and breadth. Whether for Bible student, pastor, or counselor, the authors have unlocked the treasures of Lamentations to preaching and teaching the text of this extraordinary prophet. Multiple outlines, study guides, and insights for counseling provide unique entrées into understanding the text, making this a must-have tool for every library.

—Irv Busenitz
Vice President for Academic Administration
Professor of Bible Exposition and Old Testament
The Master's Seminary

GOD'S MERCY
IN OUR
SUFFERING

Eric Kress and Paul Tautges

KRESS
BIBLICAL
RESOURCES

God's Mercy in Our Suffering
Published by Kress Biblical
Resources PO Box 132228
The Woodlands, TX 77393
Originally published in 2010 as *The Discipline of Mercy*

All Scripture quotations, unless otherwise indicated, are taken from the New American Standard
Bible®. © Copyright The Lockman Foundation 1960, 1962, 1963, 1968, 1971, 1972, 1973,
1975, 1977, 1995. Used by permission. (www.Lockman.org). Scripture quotations marked (NLT)
are taken from the Holy Bible, New Living Translation, copyright © 1996. Used by permission
of Tyndale House Publishers Inc., Wheaton, Illinois 60189. All rights reserved. Scripture
quotations marked (NET) are from the NET Bible®, copyright © 1996–2005 by Biblical Studies
Press LLC, www.bible.org. Used by permission. All rights reserved. Scripture quotations marked
(YLT) are taken from *Young's Literal Translation*.

Italics in Scripture quotations reflect the author's added emphasis.

ISBN 978-1-934952-50-4

Copyright © 2010, 2019 by Eric E. Kress and Paul K. Tautges

Interior design by Katherine Lloyd, www.TheDESKonline.com

Printed in the United States of America
10 9 8 7 6 5 4 3 2 1

CONTENTS

INTRODUCTION

As we open the neglected book of Lamentations, we may imagine the prophet Jeremiah[1] sitting on a hillside outside Jerusalem, overwhelmed by grief—*weeping*—as he remembers the glory of a city now in ruins. Undoubtedly, his mind's eye still sees the city wall, its towers, its palace, and the incomparable beauty of Solomon's temple. Perhaps Jeremiah is also reflecting on the forty years he preached throughout Judah, warning the people of the judgment God had promised if they continued in their defiance against the authority of His Word as proclaimed by His prophets. Despite beatings, opposition, and imprisonment, this spokesman for God had fulfilled his calling by preaching against the idolatrous people, disobedient priests, corrupt civil leaders, and false prophets—choosing to trust the Lord rather than men (Jeremiah 17:5–8).

This calling from God came to Jeremiah while he was still very young. In fact, he was ordained by God as a prophet while yet in his mother's womb (Jeremiah 1:5, 10). During his long ministry, Jeremiah spoke for God by warning the people of the impending threat of judgment if they refused to repent. Consider one example:

> "I will give over Zedekiah king of Judah and his servants and the people, even those who survive in this city from the pestilence, the sword and the famine, into the hand of Nebuchadnezzar king of Babylon, and into the

---

1 According to 2 Chronicles 35:25, Jeremiah was known as the author of a noncanonical book of lamentations, written after Josiah's death some twenty years earlier. There are also many similarities of expression between the book of Lamentations and the book of Jeremiah (cf. Lamentations 1:2 with Jeremiah 30:14; Lamentations 1:16; 2:11, 18; 3:48 with Jeremiah 9:1, 18; 13:17; 14:17–22; Lamentations 2:20; 4:10 with Jeremiah 19:9; and Lamentations 4:21 with Jeremiah 49:12; see also the comparison between Lamentations 2:22 with Jeremiah 6:25; 20:3, 10; 46:5; 49:5, 29; Lamentations 3:14 with Jeremiah 20:7—taken from *Constable's Expository Notes on the Bible* and Walter C. Kaiser. *Grief and Pain in the Plan of God* (Fearn: Christian Focus, 2004), 27).

hand of their foes and into the hand of those who seek their lives; and he will strike them down with the edge of the sword." (Jeremiah 21:7)

The capture of the city, its king, and its people is described in detail in Jeremiah 39:1–11. After eighteen exhausting months of warfare, the city fell to the king of Babylon. Zedekiah, king of Judah, attempted to flee but was easily caught by Nebuchadnezzar, who then executed Zedekiah's sons before their father's eyes, which were then plucked out before binding him in bronze shackles and hauling him off to Babylon while the Chaldeans burned the city. So devastating was the destruction of the cherished city, and so shameful was Judah's defeat, that the Jews have made it a practice to read the book of Lamentations once every year, in mid-July, so that they will never forget the day their great city fell.

Jerusalem's destruction had been predicted eight hundred years earlier: "When you transgress the covenant of the Lord your God, which He commanded you, and go and serve other gods and bow down to them, then the anger of the Lord will burn against you, and you will perish quickly from off the good land which He has given you" (Joshua 23:16). Jeremiah had also predicted its destruction for forty years, for which he was scorned and mistreated. The people did not want to hear God's truth, as is often the case even now. It is difficult for people to listen to warnings of impending judgment.

Unlike the false prophets, who preached only cheery messages of false hope, and who contradicted God's promise of captivity, Jeremiah endured to an unpopular end. The faithful prophet's message was simple: "'Return, faithless Israel,' declares the Lord; 'I will not look upon you in anger'" (Jeremiah 3:12). "Repent, people of God. Return to the Lord," was his message. But they closed their ears, refusing to listen to God's servant. Consequently, they "made their faces harder than rock" and continued to commit spiritual adultery with false gods (5:3–7; 6:10). It's no wonder Jeremiah has earned the nickname "The Weeping Prophet." Little did he know, a ministry characterized by such loneliness was preparing him for a worse day—a day that held deeper grief than he had ever imagined.

Now, about forty years after his initial call, Jeremiah reflects on all that has happened and writes five funeral dirges in memory of his beloved city. These mournful poems, comprising the book of Lamentations, were written after the fall of Jerusalem to Nebuchadnezzar in 587 BC and before the prophet was forced to move to Egypt (Jeremiah 43:1–7), where, according to Jewish tradition, he died.

The original audience who received Jeremiah's dirge was the generation of Jewish peoples who survived the destruction of Jerusalem. For the inspired historical accounts of what they experienced, we may look to 2 Kings 25; 2 Chronicles 36:11–21; and Jeremiah 39–40 (see also Ezekiel 24; Zechariah 7:3, 5; 8:19—cf. Leviticus 26:14–33; Deuteronomy 28:15–57; 32:15–43). The generation that experienced this ruin had been self-deceived, trusting in their religion instead of in Yahweh (Jeremiah 7:3–15).

The book of Lamentations was written as a testimony to the sovereign faithfulness of God in judgment and the enduring mercies of God in the face of overwhelming pain, grief, sorrow, despair, and devastation. It would help the survivors cope with the horrendous consequences they no doubt had to deal with. It would be used for generations to come to memorialize the destruction of the Temple (and, in God's providence, the destruction that came at the hands of the Romans in AD 70 was on the same calendar day as the Babylonian destruction). It would give subsequent generations a model of how to deal with the consequences of sin on both a national and personal level. And it would remind all those who read or heard it of the horrifying consequences of sin and covenant unfaithfulness.

Millennia later, Jeremiah's lament continues to lead God's people on the painful but sure path to the faithful mercies of Israel's God. We, like Jeremiah, have to live with the temporal consequences of sin in a fallen world. How do we deal with sin's devastation all around us? We must begin to see the difficult circumstances as God's discipline or training rather than the dealings of blind fate (Hebrews 12:5–11). We must yield to the discipleship of Jeremiah—who spoke with compassion, yet clarity and realism, about the consequences of sin and who counseled a relentless pursuit of the Lord.

After almost thirty years of pastoral ministry, I (Paul) have learned that too many people don't like to be counseled in the manner Jeremiah prescribed. However, my role as a preacher requires me to warn people of the judgment that will come if they refuse to repent. As a counselor, I must sometimes tell others that "a little bit of emergency counseling" will not solve their problems. Instead, I must warn them that things may get worse—sometimes much worse—before they get better. That is not a popular message, but it is often true. When we finally get serious about turning away from our sin and following after God, our way may be difficult for a long time as the Holy Spirit exposes the cancerous sin in our hearts—sin we must honestly face if we want to avoid death.

In truth, all suffering is ultimately caused by sin—individual, corporate, or simply the residual effects of Adam and Eve's sin. At times in our life, we will be faced with the task of comforting the sufferer. At other times, we will be the sufferer. In fact, the believer's greatest pain comes in dealing with the consequences of unfaithfulness and sin—whether one's own or someone else's.

When we find ourselves here—and we will—Lamentations is our handbook. In this biblical record, we are exhorted to place our hope fully in the faithful mercy and loyal love of a gracious God, to praise and take refuge in God, no matter the suffering. He alone is sovereign and rules forever. His mercies are new every morning, and His faithfulness is unfathomably great. No other book of the Bible, except Job, so unabashedly addresses the issue of suffering. And in a unique sense, Lamentations tackles the painful issues of suffering that are caused as the direct consequence of sin.

We might humbly summarize God's great design in including this magnificent book in His Scriptures with the following four statements of purpose:

1. To reveal the horror, tragedy, pain, sorrow, and devastation that results from sin (see entire book, but especially 1:5, 14, 18–19, 22; 2:14; 3:42; 4:13–16, 22a; 5:16–18).

Sin does not deliver on its promises. Rather, it brings only pain and misery with its rebellion. Sin's pleasure is only for a moment. Moses knew this and therefore did not consider "the passing pleasures of sin" or the "treasures of Egypt" to be ultimately worthwhile (Hebrews 11:25–26). Sin delivers hardship, misery, and pain. James 1:14–15 records the gestation cycle of sin and its horrifying consequences: "But each one is tempted when he is carried away and enticed by his own lust. Then when lust has conceived, it gives birth to sin; and when sin is accomplished, it brings forth death." The book of Lamentations graphically pictures the deadly consequences of sin. As Charles Swindoll writes:

It [Lamentations] is a mute reminder that sin, in spite of all its allurement and excitement, carries with it heavy weights of sorrow, grief, misery, barrenness, and pain. It is the other side of the "eat, drink, and be merry coin."[2]

As heinous as some of the scenes poetically captured in Lamentations are, the *eternal* consequences of sin are indescribably worse. The wages of sin is eternal destruction, "away from the presence of the Lord and from the glory of His power" (2 Thessalonians 1:9). It will be a place where the worm never dies and the fire is never quenched—indeed, a place of eternal destruction (Mark 9:48; Revelation 20:10, 15). Lamentations is but an earthly picture of the consequences of sin; the reality of the eternal consequences is much worse. But the graphic and grotesque consequences of sin disclosed in the book of Lamentations only serve to highlight the wondrous truth revealed in Matthew 1:21, as the angel announced the arrival of Messiah to Joseph: "She will bear a Son; and you shall call His name Jesus, for He will save His people from their sins" (see also 1 John 3:5). This is the hope of the gospel—the hope Jesus was sent to bring to sinners like us.

2. To reveal the hope that is found in God—His faithfulness, His love, and His mercy in the midst of such consequences (3:19–38, 54–66; and by implication 1:9b, 11b, 20; 2:20; 3:39–66; 4:22; 5:1, 19–22).

Jeremiah chose a highly stylized method of recording this book of sorrows. He composed five individual songs of sorrow, which correspond to our five chapters. The poetry of each of the first four chapters follows an alphabetic acrostic form with some slight variations (Psalm 119 is an example of poetry done in acrostic form).

Chapter 1 is comprised of twenty-two verses with sixty-six lines, each verse beginning with the corresponding letter of the Hebrew alphabet (e.g., v. 1—"Ah, lonely sits…"; v. 2—"Bewailing she wails…"; v. 3—"Captive is Judah…"). The general meter is in a 3 + 2 pattern, resulting in a halting rhythm that would accentuate the words and identify it as a funeral lament. As Dyer writes, "This

---

2   Charles R. Swindoll. *The Lamentations of Jeremiah*, "Introduction," quoted in *Constable's Expository Notes on the Bible* (Garland: Galaxie Software).

forms a 3 + 2 'limping meter which conveys a hollow, incomplete feeling to the reader. Both of these elements lend an air of sadness to the dirges and heighten their emotional intensity."[3]

Like the first poem, chapter 2 is comprised of twenty-two verses with sixty-six lines, following the same acrostic pattern—except that the Hebrew letters corresponding to *O* and *P* in our English alphabet are transposed.[4] As Dyer explains:

In each of chapters 2–4, two of the Hebrew letters are reversed. The normal order of the Hebrew alphabet for the 16th and 17th letters is *ayin-pe* (cf. Ps. 119). This is the order given in Lamentations 1. However, in Lamentations 2–4 this order is reversed, giving a *pe-ayin* sequence. This reversal perplexed scholars for many years, but recent archeological discoveries have helped clear up the difficulty. Several Hebrew abecedaries (alphabets scratched on pieces of broken pottery by Hebrew children learning to write) have been found by archeologists. Some of these alphabetical lists are in the normal order for the Hebrew letters but others are in the reverse *pe-ayin* order. Evidently both arrangements of the alphabet were acceptable. Thus the writer of Lamentations was merely employing two forms of the Hebrew alphabet, both of which were used in his time.[5]

Chapter 3 is comprised of sixty-six verses, but still with sixty-six lines. The alphabetic acrostic in chapter 3 corresponds with the Hebrew alphabet, except in triplets (a, a, a, b, b, b, c, c, c, etc.; i.e., v. 1—"Affliction by the rod"; v. 2—"And in darkness, not in light"; v. 3—"All the day"; v. 4—"Bones of mine"; v. 5—"Bitterness and distress"; v. 6—"Buried in dark places"[6]).

Chapter 4 returns to the twenty-two-verse format, but this time with only forty-four lines. The acrostic pattern is used here as well.

---

3 Charles H. Dyer in Roy B. Zuck and John F. Walvoord, eds. *The Bible Knowledge Commentary* (Wheaton: Victor Books, 1985), 1210.

4 Kaiser, 13.

5 Dyer, 1210–11.

6 See Irving L. Jensen. *Jeremiah and Lamentations* (Everyman's Bible Commentary) (Chicago: Moody, 1974), 123.

Chapter 5 has twenty-two verses and again forty-four lines but has no acrostic pattern.

The overall structure of the book of Lamentations then points to chapter 3 as the centerpiece, as the first two chapters build up to it. The final two chapters lessen in intensity from the crescendo of chapter 3 and seem to communicate a continued processing of the pain so intensely described in the first two chapters. Chapter 5 ends with a prayer of humble affirmation and petition for restoration (vv. 19–20).

There is only one real help in suffering. There is only one genuine hope for those who know their utter hopelessness—*God Himself.* Looking in faith to God is the only lasting comfort in sorrow. Even if worship is washed in tears of grief, worship is the only proper response to pain. The book of Lamentations leads us to that conclusion.

3. To reveal the sovereign faithfulness of God in both judgment and mercy—His hatred of sin, His holy wrath, and His loyal love (1:12b–15, 18; 2:1–8, 17; 3:21–26, 37–38, 54–66; 4:11, 16, 22; 5:19; cf. Leviticus 26:14–33; Deuteronomy 28:15–57; 32:15–43).

It is interesting to note that Babylon and the Babylonians are never mentioned in Lamentations. Only Edom is cited as an adversary (4:21–22). The perspective of this book clearly leads to the conclusion that God was ultimately sovereign over the horrendous events that happened. Certainly the Bible teaches that God is not the source of evil, but Lamentations stresses that He is sovereign over it—and will use the evil of men to accomplish His purposes. It is precisely because God is sovereign that His disciplined and grieving people can have hope in the midst of pain and tragic circumstances.

4. To foster prayer and worship in the face of tragedy, pain, sorrow, and devastation—and increase our anticipation of the glory to come (cf. point 2 above; see also all of chapter 5).

The final song, found in chapter 5, is a prayer. Lamentations should help us understand how we can pray and worship in the face of devastation—even the devastation of sin and its consequences. And worship is man's deepest need, highest joy, and everlasting privilege. Such worship will thus help the sufferer process the grief, horror, and pain of sin's consequences—until the God of all comfort wipes away every tear from our eyes (Revelation 21:1ff).

How to Use This Book

This book is designed to be helpful for a wide range of readers seeking to access the wisdom of God contained in Lamentations. For *the Bible student,* this book complements a study of Lamentations at any depth. For *the expositor,* you have at your fingertips an expositional commentary loaded with application as well as research. For *the biblical counselor,* the final section of each chapter includes a set of principles designed for the soul work you are doing—applying the Word of God to the lives of those to whom you minister. A complete set of ready-made homework assignments for your counselees is also included. A list of essential reading is also included at the end of the book. For *the small group leader,* a comprehensive study guide, suitable for discussion and/or individual study, is provided at the end of the book.

Note to Biblical Counselors

It's essential to begin teaching your counselees this truth: Now that they are believers in Christ, they need to discipline themselves to reorient every part of their lives under 2 Corinthians 5:14–15: "For the love of Christ controls us, having concluded this, that one died for all, therefore all died; and He died for all, so that they who live might no longer live for themselves, but for Him who died and rose again on their behalf." Help them to understand that the saving gospel of Christ provides not only security for eternity (as substantial as that is), but also empowers them to exchange their self-centeredness for the joy of living for the One who died and rose again.

Teach your counselees (those you are discipling for the Lord) the practice of preaching the gospel to themselves every day as they learn to put off the old life and put on the new (Ephesians 4:17–32).[7] An excellent resource is *A Gospel Primer for Christians* by Milton Vincent.[8] Make regular reading of portions of this small and extremely helpful book part of your homework assignments.

---

7 For development of this principle see Jerry Bridges, *The Gospel for Real Life* (Colorado Springs: Nav Press, 2003), and Jerry Bridges, *The Discipline of Grace* (Colorado Springs: Nav Press, 2006).

8 Milton Vincent, *A Gospel Primer for Christians* (Bemidji, MN: Focus Publishing, 2008). Available from www.focuspublishing.com.

Chapter 1

"SEE, O LORD!"

A Song of Sorrow and Despair

Lamentations 1:1–22

As he looks upon the smoking rubble of Jerusalem, Jeremiah wonders, *Does anyone care? Does anybody care what we've been through? Does anyone really know the depth of my grief and pain?* Six times in this chapter, the loneliness of the empty city is expressed: "She has no one to comfort her" (v. 2); "She has no comforter" (v. 9); "Is it [our pain and suffering] nothing to all you who pass this way?" (v. 12); "…far from me is a comforter" (v. 16); "There is no one to comfort her" (v. 17); and finally, the city, personified as a woman, says, "There is no one to comfort me" (v. 21).

It can be that way for us too. When we find ourselves experiencing correction from the hand of our loving God, we often feel alone and are tempted to ask, "Does anyone really care?"

Where can we go when drowning in the pain, grief, loneliness, and shame of sin's consequences? The book of Lamentations addresses this issue plainly yet poetically. It reveals that we can be unflinchingly honest in our prayers and in our assessment of our circumstances. We can speak emotionally. Yet in the midst of the emotion, we must seek God to somehow cope with the pain. He alone is the key to finding mercy in the midst of misery.

God is faithful not only to chastise His people in order to save us from the eternal condemnation of sin, but also to walk through our suffering with us. God loves His own too much not to discipline us, and He also loves us too much to abandon us in the midst of His discipline. Instead, He is faithful to suffer with His people, cleansing us, healing us, and grieving with us for the purpose of molding us into useful vessels for His glory.

In Lamentations 1:1–22, we will see four movements in this first song of sorrow that will help us process the pain and loneliness that comes as a result of sin.

TEACHING OUTLINES

Option A

I. A song of sorrow and despair (vv. 1–22)

    A. Chronicling the pain of loneliness and loss (vv. 1–7)

        1. No position (v. 1)

        2. No lovers (v. 2)

        3. No rest (v. 3)

        4. No joy (v. 4)

        5. No freedom (v. 5)

        6. No strength (v. 6)

        7. No testimony—nothing but memories (v. 7)

    B. Clarifying its causes from a human standpoint—sin and uncleanness (vv. 8–11)

        1. Sin led to dishonor and shame (v. 8)

        2. Sin led to despair and shocking failure (v. 9)

        3. Sin led to defilement and sacrilege (v. 10)

        4. Sin led to desperation and starvation (v. 11)

    C. Clarifying its causes from the divine standpoint—divine judgment (vv. 12–17)

        1. The LORD's fierce anger (v. 12)

        2. The LORD's merciful discipline (v. 13)

        3. The LORD's sovereign judgment (v. 14)

        4. The LORD's sovereign humbling (vv. 15–17)

            a. The appointed time of judgment (v. 15)

   b. The agony and tears (v. 16)

   c. The adversaries decreed by Yahweh (v. 17)

  D. Confessing sin and calling for covenant mercy/faithfulness (vv. 18–22)

   1. The LORD is righteous for I have rebelled against His command (v. 18)

   2. The lovers I trusted in deceived me (v. 19)

   3. The look of the LORD is my only hope in the midst of sin's consequences (v. 20)

   4. The longing I have is for God's covenant faithfulness to be expressed (vv. 21–22)

    a. The folly of Israel's enemies (v. 21a)

    b. The faithfulness of God (v. 21b–22)

Option B

I. A Portrait of Misery (vv. 1–11)

  A. Characteristics of the misery (vv. 1–7)

   1. Financial reversal (v. 1)

   2. Desertion by friends (v. 2)

   3. Servitude without rest (v. 3)

   4. Heavy sadness (v. 4)

   5. Bondage to adversaries (v. 5)

   6. Fear and hopelessness (v. 6)

   7. Bitter regret (v. 7)

  B. Cause of the misery (vv. 8–11)

II. A Plea for Mercy (vv. 12–22)

  A. Right thinking about sin (vv. 12–17)

   1. My sin has provoked God's anger (v. 12)

   2. My sin has sapped me of strength (vv. 13–15)

   3. My sin has brought much shame (vv. 16–17)

  B. Right thinking about God (vv. 18–22)

   1. God is right to discipline me (v. 18)

   2. God is the only true satisfier (v. 19)

   3. God sees me in my distress (v. 20)

   4. God will judge all sin righteously (vv. 21–22)

EXPOSITION
VERSE 1

How lonely sits the city that was full of people!

Verse 1 emphasizes the contrast between what had been and the current pain-ful reality. As Jeremiah looks at the city, once a bustling marketplace filled with people going to and from the Temple for worship, he now sees nothing but emptiness. The word here translated "how" is an exclamation that also begins chapters 2 and 4 (2:1; 4:1). It is used rhetorically to reference incredible, even tragic circumstances (see Isaiah 1:21; Jeremiah 48:17). The NET Bible translates it "Alas!"—a cry of lament. "It is an exclamation of shock, an incredulous gasp behind which lurks a question: how ever did this change come about?"[1]

The word *lonely* can be translated "alone" or "solitary." Jeremiah recounts that Jerusalem was once a very populated "city...full of people." But now it sits nearly deserted, a solitary place, isolated like a leper from the rest of humanity (Leviticus 13:46). "In normal times Jerusalem, Judah's capital, was a bustling commercial center as well as the focal point of national cultic worship. Now she is a deserted ruin, stripped of all her former grandeur and emptied of her inhabitants."[2]

She has become like a widow who was once great among the nations!

Widow in Jeremiah's culture was synonymous with difficulty, loneliness, poverty, and hardship (see Deuteronomy 24:17; Isaiah 1:23). Jerusalem "was once great among the nations"; now, however, "she has become like a widow"—"destitute and defenseless"[3] (cf. Psalm 94:6; Isaiah 10:2; Malachi 3:5). She does not know how to deal with her loneliness; she is overtaken by it. Greatness has turned to vulnerability, grief, reproach, difficulty, poverty, and hardship.

She who was a princess among the provinces has become a forced laborer!

Jerusalem has lost all prestige and position. She was a "princess among the prov-inces," but is now a slave, "a forced laborer," one who must pay tribute to a master. From royalty to rags, her fortune has been reversed. This newly widowed

---

1 John L. Mackay. *Lamentations: A Mentor Commentary* (Fearn: Christian Focus, 2008), 40.

2 R. K. Harrison *Jeremiah & Lamentations* (Downers Grove, IL: IVP, 1973), 207

3 Charles H. Dyer in Roy B. Zuck and John F. Walvoord, eds. *The Bible Knowledge Commentary* (Wheaton, IL: Victor Books, 1985), 1212.

one is alone, empty, and poor. In Solomon's day, Jerusalem was the greatest city on earth; now, in Jeremiah's time, it is a slave paying tribute to Gentiles.

Jeremiah sings a song of pain and lament over Jerusalem's loss of position, place, and prestige in the world.

Verse 2

She weeps bitterly in the night / and her tears are on her cheeks

This could be translated, "Weeping she weeps in the night; and the tears are on her cheeks." The isolation, grief, and pain are depicted as sleeplessness, continual sobbing, and tears. Instead of the normal progression of weeping giving way to sleep, here there is no mention of sleep.

She has none to comfort her / among all her lovers / all her friends have dealt treacherously with her

The utter lack of any consolation or comforter is a resounding theme in this chapter as seen by the use of the same term in 1:9, 16, 17, and 21. *All* is used sixteen times in this chapter (1:2, 3, 4, 6, 7, 8, 10, 11, 12, 13, 15, 18, 21, 22) to emphasize the total devastation. "She cannot discern any ray of light in the gloom of her depression."[4]

The idea of Israel's illicit "lovers" is also seen in Jeremiah 2:20–3:2 (see also Jeremiah 4:30; 22:20–22; 30:14; Ezekiel 16:35–41; 23:22–49; Hosea 2:7.) These lovers were the idols and nations Israel trusted in rather than Yahweh, the true and living God. Those she believed to be friends were in fact unfaithful to her. They betrayed her. Weeping, she finds no comfort in her false gods.

Her idols fail to satisfy and ultimately forsake her. Israel has now learned this lesson the hard way—through degradation, sleeplessness, sobbing, and tears. There is "none to comfort her." All her military alliances are useless. They too have abandoned her and have even "dealt treacherously with her." She has been deserted by those she trusted most.

---

4 Mackay, 44.

VERSE 3

Judah has gone into exile under affliction / and under harsh servitude

From Jerusalem, Jeremiah moves on to speak of Judah, a nation that had "gone into exile under affliction / and under harsh servitude." The term *affliction* was used of Israel's suffering in Egypt before the Exodus (Exodus 3:17), as with the term *servitude* (1:14). She is back under bondage, without rest or peace.

She dwells among the nations, but she has found no rest

The nation was scattered "among the [Gentile] nations." In the days of Moses and Joshua, *rest* was equated with Israel living in the Promised Land (Deuteronomy 12:10; 25:19; Joshua 1:13; 21:44; 23:1; 1 Kings 8:56; Psalm 95). But after the fall of Jerusalem, Israel "found no rest" (see the promises of Leviticus 26:33–38; Deuteronomy 28:64–67; Joshua 23:11–16).

All her pursuers have overtaken her / in the midst of distress

The word *distress* means literally "narrow places." The language pictures a fleeing Judah seeking to escape but being overtaken in a narrow place. The troublesome nightmare has become a reality. The carefree princess is now a slave whose life is filled with anxiety.

There is no rest—only capture, exile, affliction, and great servitude.

VERSE 4

The roads of Zion are in mourning / because no one comes to the appointed feasts

Zion had become synonymous with Jerusalem, but properly speaking, it referred to the hill of the LORD, where the Temple sat—the house of God (Psalm 2:6; 68:16). That seems to be the distinction here. Jerusalem is a widow, Judah a captive, and the Temple mount embittered because of loneliness and desolation. Poetically the "roads of Zion" are personified as mourning because of the want of people coming to partake of "the appointed" worship prescribed by the Law of Moses. The roads of Jerusalem, once occupied by those coming to celebrate the feasts of the Lord, are now empty because the temple is gone, reduced to a pile of smoking bricks.

*All her gates are desolate; her priests are groaning, her virgins
are afflicted, and she herself is bitter*

The "gates" of the Temple were "desolate," empty and ruined (cf. 1:13, 16; 3:11; 4:5; 5:18). The Temple "priests" are sighing, groaning (cf. 1:8, 1, 21 for "groan"), the loss and emptiness seemingly unbearable. The Temple "virgins" (or "young women") may have had some role in worship, as Jeremiah 31:13–14 and Joel 1:8–9 indicate. Psalm 68:25 says, "The singers went on, the musicians after them, in the midst of the *maidens* beating tambourines." The "virgins" were "suffering/afflicted," which speaks of "grief" (1:5; 3:32–33) and even "torment" (Job 19:2; Isaiah 51:23).

Finally, Judah "herself is bitter" or, better translated, "suffers bitterly" in the depths of grief. She carries a heavy burden on her shoulders: the loss of joy and worship. There is no more position, power, or prestige; no more friends or worldly lovers; no more rest; and no more joy.

VERSE 5

Her adversaries have become her masters, her enemies prosper

Not only have her friends become her enemies, but those enemies have also enslaved her. She is in deep bondage. This could be translated, "Her distressors have become for [her] the head; the ones hostile to her are at ease" (see specifically Deuteronomy 28:13, 43–44). Babylon and its rulers became the head and appeared to be "at ease."

*For the Lord has caused her grief / because of the multitude
of her transgressions*

This is the first acknowledgment in this song of sorrow concerning the cause of Israel's pain. Jeremiah records the name "Yahweh" here for the first time as well. Israel's faithful, covenant-keeping, loyal God—the ever-living One—had "caused her grief." The reason? "Because of the multitude of her transgressions." The NET Bible renders this phrase, "For her many acts of rebellion."

While not all suffering is a direct result of personal sin, it is related to mankind's rebellion against God. Jeremiah will deal with this in greater detail in verses 8–11 and even more extensively in chapter 2. But here he briefly records it while detailing the loneliness and loss in Jerusalem, Judah, and Zion.

Her little ones have gone away / as captives before the adversary

Captivity had been foretold in Deuteronomy 28:36, 62–68. Not even their "little ones," their children, have the prospect of freedom. They "have gone away as captives before the adversary." It is one thing to be a slave yourself, but quite another to see your children taken as slaves to a foreign land, never to be seen again. Families and lives were shattered beyond comprehension.

Jeremiah lamented the loss of freedom as a result of sin. And it reached to even the "little ones."

Verse 6

All her majesty / has departed from the daughter of Zion

The word *majesty* can speak of "splendor" but also of "honor" and "dignity." "The daughter of Zion" would seem to again refer to Jerusalem and, by extension, all of Judah and Israel. She is no doubt afraid about the future and suffers from despair. There is hopelessness—all has been lost; all has been destroyed. The next phrase reveals that Jeremiah was thinking of the splendor, honor, and dignity of Judah's monarchy. It too is now gone.

Her princes have become like deer / that have found no pasture; and they have fled without strength / before the pursuer

See Jeremiah 52:6–11 (cf. 2 Kings 25:3–7). See also Lamentations 5:12. The NLT translates this as, "Her princes are like starving deer searching for pasture. They are too weak to run from the pursuing enemy."

Verse 7

In the days of her affliction and homelessness / Jerusalem remembers all her precious things / that were from the days of old

Here, finally, Jeremiah uses the common name of "Jerusalem." The root term here translated *homelessness* is rendered "wandering" in 3:19. The "precious things" refer to the articles of the Temple in 1:10 and 2 Chronicles 36:19, which were taken to Babylon. That which was used to honor the LORD is now gone. These worship treasures are now merely a memory as all Jerusalem suffers from bitter regret.

When her people fell into the hand of the adversary / and no one
helped her / the adversaries saw her, they mocked at her ruin

No one came to Jerusalem's aid. All her allies abandoned her; they "mocked" her in the midst of her desperate condition. "Ha! She deserves it!" was their cry. The word *ruin* is related to the word "Sabbath." It speaks of "cessation." The thought seems to be that though Jerusalem remembers the "precious things" of Temple worship, she also remembers the "mocking" that occurred when the worship ceased. The city of Yahweh, the Temple of Yahweh, the worship of Yahweh became a laughing matter to Israel's enemies. This graphic description of misery leads to the conclusion that, from the princes to the people, all has been destroyed. All is lost. Nothing is left except the empty loneliness and enslavement that characterizes a bitter life. But what was the cause of such misery?

VERSE 8

Jerusalem sinned greatly / therefore she has become an unclean thing

This could be translated, "Sinning Jerusalem sinned, thus she became an object of mockery." While the cause of Judah's desperate suffering has already been revealed in verse 5—"For the LORD has caused her grief because of the multitude of her transgressions"—here Jeremiah clearly and emphatically clarifies the human cause of the pain that he has chronicled—"sin," failure to live by faith and honor God. It was the southern kingdom's defiance against God's Word that brought such miserable conditions upon her. Sin led to dishonor and shame.

The root for "unclean thing" may be related to menstrual impurity.[5] The NLT renders this phrase: "Jerusalem has sinned greatly, so she has been tossed away like a filthy rag." The context seems to support such an understanding.

All who honored her despise her / because they have
seen her nakedness

The nations once "honored" or "glorified" Israel (1 Kings 10:4–29). Even Babylon had come to admire her in Hezekiah's day (Isaiah 39:2). Now they

---

5   R. Laird Harris, editor, *Theological Wordbook of the Old Testament* (Chicago, Moody Press, 1980).

"despise her"—treat her lightly and consider her worthless. The picture Jeremiah's words depict is of a prostitute. Jerusalem had been stripped naked for the entire world to behold her filthiness. We see this representation in Ezekiel 16 as well. Jerusalem sinned greatly, and as a result, she who was once smug in her rebellion is now filled with self-loathing. She is ashamed of herself and weeps.

Even she herself groans and turns away

The sight of Jerusalem's sin was so disgusting that when it was exposed, it was unbearable to look at. As Laetsch remarks: "Stripped naked of all her splendor, only filth is seen (cf. Ezekiel 16:1–43), filth so horrible, and nudeness so abhorrent, that not only her former admirers despise her (v. 8), but she herself moans and turns her back in shame, aghast at her own ugliness."[6]

VERSE 9

Her uncleanness was in her skirts

Jeremiah speaks of sin as the stain of menstruation, or an unclean discharge in the skirts of a prostitute. The horrible scene is one of an illicit woman being stripped in the sight of all with the pollution in her skirt evident to all. The language is poetic but brutally blunt.

She did not consider her future / therefore she has fallen astonishingly

She once enjoyed her sin without any thought of future consequences. She sinned without limit, giving no thought to the painful consequences it was sure to deliver. Jeremiah here seems to be referencing a line from the song of Moses, which was to be a warning and testimony to Israel concerning apostasy and its consequences: "Would that they were wise, that they understood this, that they would discern their future!" (Deuteronomy 32:29, though the warning may have first referenced Israel's enemies in the context of Moses' song). Again, the NLT is provocative: "She defiled herself with immorality and gave no thought to her future. Now she lies in the gutter with no one to lift her out."

---

6 Theo Laetsch. *Jeremiah* (St. Louis: Concordia, 1952), 379–80.

She has no comforter

This exact phrase is also used in verses 17 and 21. Lying in the gutter, exposed for what she is, the fallen woman "has no comforter." Only God and His promises can serve as an adequate comforter (cf. Jeremiah 31:13). Thus, comfortless, the remnant of faith cries out to God in the next phrase.

"See, O LORD, my affliction, for the enemy has magnified himself!"

Moving abruptly from third person to a startling direct address, Jeremiah pens a prayer of fledgling faith on behalf of the fallen city: "See, O LORD, my suffering." Judah is crying out, "See what I have done to my life. See what the enemy has accomplished as he has 'magnified himself,' through the deceitfulness of my sin!" Even in her low estate, Judah knows that the merciful "look" of Yahweh is her only hope. The final phrase, "for the enemy has magnified himself," assumes a level of faith in the Abrahamic promises of Genesis 12:3: "I will bless those who bless you and him who dishonors you will I curse."

VERSE 10

The adversary has stretched out his hand / over all her precious things, for she has seen the nations enter her sanctuary

The mention of "precious things" and "sanctuary" most likely alludes to the Temple. See Jeremiah 52:17–20 (cf. Psalm 74; 79; Isaiah 64:10–12; Jeremiah 15:13–14; 20:5; Ezekiel 7:22). Judah must stand by and watch as the enemies enter the Temple and plunder everything sacred.

The ones whom You commanded / that they should not enter into Your congregation

According to Deuteronomy 23:3, Ammonites and Moabites were forbidden from entering the Temple. There may have been troops from these nations within the Babylonian coalition army. In fact, 2 Kings 24:2 confirms that they were present in earlier forays against Judah. Deuteronomy 23:7–8 indicates that first- or second-generation Edomites were forbidden as well, and they likely helped to loot and destroy the Temple. Jeremiah 51:51 reads: "We are ashamed because we have heard reproach; disgrace has covered our faces, for aliens have entered the holy places of the LORD's house" (cf. Nehemiah 13:3; Ezekiel 44:7, 9).

Sin led to a complete and total corruption of worship, as her enemies have entered her "sanctuary," the Temple, and have carried the treasures away to idolatrous Babylon (cf. Daniel 1:1–2). Israel had already defiled Jerusalem and the sanctuary (Ezekiel 5:10–11; 8:10–18; 23:29), and God, in judgment, brought it to completion (Ezekiel 9:6–10).

VERSE 11

All her people groan seeking bread; they have given their precious things for food / to restore their lives themselves

She who was once rich is now begging for bread. She has sold all that she has (the term "precious things" is used again, this time evidently referring to prized personal possessions) simply to buy food. Perhaps there is an ironic twist to the people selling their charms and prized idols for "food to restore their lives themselves." Second Kings 25:3 says, "On the ninth day of the fourth month the famine was so severe in the city that there was no food for the people of the land." Some suggest that the term "precious things" here is a reference to their own children[7] (cf. Hosea 9:16 for a parallel). Evidently, "life was an unremitting search for bread…the city gates might be open, but the surrounding land had been devastated by the invading armies, and the farm labourers had been slain or enslaved. And agricultural economy would take years to recover from such an invasion."[8]

"See, O LORD, and look, for I am despised"

A second time, Jeremiah abruptly shifts from third to first person to utter a prayer on behalf of Jerusalem's remnant, invoking a plea for Yahweh, the faithful, covenant-keeping God of love and justice, to "see" and "look" with regard and pity. The phrase "for I am despised" speaks of a worthless condition. This picture of misery rightly leads the prophet to beg for God's mercy.

---

7 "Jeremiah and Lamentations" in *The Complete Biblical Library* (Springfield: World Library Press, 2000), 577.
8 Mackay, 57.

VERSE 12

"Is it nothing to all you who pass this way?"

Verses 12–22, with the exception of verse 17, switch to the first person—as if Jerusalem herself is giving account of the Lord's fierce anger against her. This difficult poetic line seems to picture Jerusalem personified as calling out to whoever passes by. It is possible to translate this phrase, "May it never happen to you!"[9] But the sentiments of verses 21–22 militate against that rendering. Here Jerusalem is focused on her own suffering and the absence of anyone to comfort her. The idea is, "Doesn't anyone care?" Perhaps the Geneva Bible captures this: "Have ye no regard, all ye that pass by this way?"

*"Look and see if there is any pain like my pain / which was
severely dealt out to me"*

Whereas verse 11 petitioned for Yahweh to "look" and "see," now it is addressed to "all you who pass this way." There may be an intended warning in these words.

We call for Yahweh to mercifully regard our distress, and we look to others to see and regard the severity of our pain and sorrow as well. "This is not too much different from what we also do in our grief. We believe what we are going through is extraordinary and totally removed from what any normal human being can bear."[10] But the description in the rest of the book merits some consideration for Jerusalem's more grievous sorrow. In fact, Daniel's prayer in Daniel 9:12 confirms the uniqueness of the divine judgment that fell upon Jerusalem in Jeremiah's day: "He has confirmed his words, which he spoke against us and against our rulers who ruled us, by bringing upon us a great calamity. For under the whole heaven there has not been done anything like what has been done against Jerusalem."

Jerusalem personified identifies the ultimate Agent behind her pain in the next phrase.

---

9 Harrison, 210.
10 Walter C. Kaiser, *Grief and Pain in the Plan of God* (Fearn: Christian Focus, 2004), 52.

"Which the Lord *inflicted on the day of His fierce anger"*

Clearly stated, it was "Yahweh" who "inflicted," or caused affliction, "on the day of His burning anger." Psalm 5:4–6 says, "For You are not a God who takes pleasure in wickedness; no evil dwells with You. The boastful shall not stand before your eyes; You hate all who do iniquity. You destroy those who speak falsehood; the Lord abhors the man of bloodshed and deceit."

Jeremiah makes no mistake about the fact that Yahweh is a God who possesses righteous, holy "burning anger" against all sin and those who rebel against Him. Proof of this divine attribute is the harsh judgment Jerusalem received on "the day" God demonstrated His wrath through the instrument of the Babylonian king. Yet for His chosen, such judgment is actually merciful discipline, as verse 13 reveals.

Verse 13

"From on high He sent fire into my bones, and it prevailed over them"

Jeremiah uses a similar expression concerning his own dealings with God in Jeremiah 20:9. Here, Jerusalem experienced the judgment of God that went to the innermost man (Psalm 11:6; see also Deuteronomy 32:22). David echoes this connection in Psalm 32:3–4: "When I kept silent about my sin, my body wasted away through my groaning all day long. For day and night Your hand was heavy upon me; my vitality was drained away as with the fever heat of summer." David acknowledges the cause of his physical degeneration—the sin he cherished by refusing to deal honestly with it. Warren Wiersbe makes an interesting connection concerning the divine fire that consumed Jerusalem: "According to the law of Moses, if a priest's daughter was guilty of immorality, she was burned to death (Leviticus 21:9). Israel was a kingdom of priests (Exodus 19:6), but she had betrayed the Lord and consorted with idols."[11]

"He has spread a net for my feet; He has turned me back"

The expression "He has spread a net for my feet" speaks of an inescapable trap. Some interpret the words "He has turned me back" as speaking of defeat—which

---

11 Warren W. Weirsbe, "Lamentations" in *The Bible Exposition Commentary* (Colorado Springs: Cook Communications, 2002), 154.

was no doubt true. But the grammar and the word itself, *turned,* can just as readily be understood as a turning in repentance.[12]

"He has made me desolate, faint all day long"

Jeremiah continues to describe sin's physical effects—a crushing of the body, mind, and spirit. The verb *made* is literally "given" (cf. v. 14). This desolation, faintness "all day long," is actually a gift from God (see Psalm 118:18 for the same form of the word). Could it be that Jeremiah wanted his audience to see such desolation and faintness as merciful?

VERSE 14

"The yoke of my transgressions is bound; by His hand they are knit together / they have come upon my neck"

The picture is of God taking all of Jerusalem's "transgressions" and making them into a "yoke," which is placed "upon [her] neck." God will not simply wink at her sin or sweep it under the rug, but rather He will employ its consequences to chasten her (see Deuteronomy 28:48). The yoke of slavery came ultimately from the hand of a sovereign God, due to sin. See also Jeremiah 28 and the ironic use of *yoke.*

The yoke will stay on the nation until that future day when Yahweh of hosts "will break his yoke from off their neck and will tear off their bonds; and strangers will no longer make them their slaves. But they shall serve the LORD their God and David their king, whom [God] will raise up for them" (Jeremiah 30:8–9).

"He has made my strength fail / the Lord has given me into the hands / of those against whom I am not able to stand"

Yes, divine judgment "made [Jerusalem's] strength fail." And *Adonai,* the Sovereign Master, gave her "into the hands of those against whom [she was] not able to stand." But in another light, such is a merciful judgment. As Kaiser writes:

> Unchecked sin can so bind its practitioners that all power to overcome it or the grip of those into whose hand such sinners eventually fall is

---

12 See Kaiser, 53.

spent and gone. Only by reducing sinners to such desperate straits will some eventually listen and turn. Thus grief may often work a very wonderful work that none of the [so-called] goodness or blessings of God will ever effect.[13]

VERSE 15

"The Lord has rejected all my strong men / in my midst"
Again, the strength of Jerusalem had been rejected. Her "strong men" were rejected by the Sovereign Master. The word *rejected* speaks of something tossed aside or something made light of. Both judgment and mercy can be detected in these words.

"He has called an appointed time against me / to crush my young men"
The "appointed time" was not for a festival in Israel, but rather for Israel's enemies to "crush [her] young men." Again, all hope of self-defense was taken away in the sovereign discipline of the Lord.

"The Lord has trodden a wine press / the virgin daughter of Judah"
See Isaiah 63:1–4 and Joel 3:13 for the imagery of the wine press of God's wrath. Here, however, the punishment is poured out on "the virgin daughter of Judah."
   The song continues in identifying the pain as coming from the sovereign hand of the Lord. It was the appointed time for judgment.

VERSE 16

"For these things I weep; my eyes run down with water"
Jeremiah 9:1 says, "Oh that my head were waters and my eyes a fountain of tears, that I might weep day and night for the slain of the daughter of my people!" (See also Isaiah 22:4; Jeremiah 8:18; 9:18; 13:17; 14:17; Lamentations 2:18.)

"Because far from me is a comforter, One who restores my soul"
The agony and tears remain because "far from [her] is a comforter, One who restores [her] soul" (cf. v. 2, 9, 17, 21). God's presence seems distant. But the

---

13 Kaiser, 53.

promise of Isaiah 66:2 remains: "But to this one I will look, to him who is humble and contrite of spirit, and who trembles at My word." And likewise Psalm 34:18: "The LORD is near to the brokenhearted, and saves those who are crushed in spirit."

"My children are desolate / because the enemy has prevailed"

The NIV renders this: "My children are destitute because the enemy has prevailed." The NLT: "My children have no future, for the enemy has conquered us." On a human level, comfort is often found in one's children. But "because the enemy [had] prevailed," there was no earthly consolation. This can only point to a heavenly comfort and Comforter (Isaiah 40:1ff).

VERSE 17

Zion stretches out her hands; there is no one to comfort her

Jeremiah briefly turns back to third person in this verse. Again, "there is no one to comfort her." This time the term *Zion* is used—either the Holy Hill or the city. Once again, human comfort is sought but none is found, as the next phrase indicates. The stretching out of hands can speak of a signal for help, as in Jeremiah 4:31.

The LORD has commanded concerning Jacob / that the ones round about him should be His adversaries

It was from the faithful, loyal, and loving decree of "Yahweh...concerning Jacob, that the ones round about him should be his adversaries." Second Kings 24:2 says, "The LORD sent against him bands of Chaldeans, bands of Arameans, bands of Moabites, and bands of Ammonites. So He sent them against Judah to destroy it, according to the word of the LORD which He had spoken through his servant the prophets." Though this was some years before the final siege and destruction, it illustrates Yahweh's sovereignty over the enemy troops sent against Jerusalem. Perhaps "Jacob" was used poetically here to refer to Israel, to hint at her forefather's preconversion nature, which she exhibited in her unbelief.

Jerusalem has become an unclean thing among them

Again the language depicts a woman in her menstrual impurity. Her cherished sin results in uncleanness, not only before God, but also among others who witness her rebellion. For the sake of worship, it rendered her and those who came in contact with her unclean (see Leviticus 15:19–30).

Verse 18

"The LORD is righteous; for I have rebelled against His command"

Immediately after directly attributing the pain to God's judgment and discipline, personified Jerusalem—once again in first person—declares, "Yahweh is righteous." Yahweh was in the right to judge so severely "because [Jerusalem had] rebelled against His command," literally "because His mouth I have disobeyed." In his larger book, Jeremiah mentions Babylon as the earthly cause of Judah's misery; however, he never names the enemy in Lamentations. Here his focus is on God as the One who is ultimately dealing with Judah's rebellion. Nebuchadnezzar and the armies of Babylon are simply God's servants—His tools of discipline.

This is the climax of this first song in Lamentations. The poet has told it like it is. He has cried and wept—detailed the pain, the sorrow, the degradation—but in the end he justifies Yahweh's righteousness in judgment and confesses Jerusalem's rebellion. Jeremiah's conclusion smacks of Job's confession in Job 42:1–6.

"Hear now, all peoples, and behold my pain; my virgins and my young men / have gone into captivity"

The call is for others to see, "behold," Jerusalem's "pain." Perhaps this is a warning to all who would disobey the mouth of the LORD. See especially Deuteronomy 28:32, 41: "Your sons and your daughters shall be given to another people, while your eyes look on and yearn for them continually; but there will be nothing you can do… You shall have sons and daughters but they will not be yours, for they will go into captivity."

Jeremiah 22:8–10 says:

Many nations will pass by this city, and they will say to one another, "Why has the LORD done thus to this great city?" Then they will answer,

"Because they forsook the covenant of the LORD their God and bowed down to other gods and served them." Do not weep for the dead or mourn for him, but weep continually for the one who goes away; for he will never return or see his native land.

Suffering, sorrow, pain, and grief can only be processed rightly when we confess and embrace that the Lord is righteous and we are sinners. A second confession/declaration is found in verse 19.

VERSE 19

"I called to my lovers, but they deceived me"
Here is an admission that *before* turning to Yahweh in confession and faith, Jerusalem had "called" to her "lovers," but "they deceived" her (see Jeremiah 30:14; 37:7–9; Hosea 2:5, 7). The nations and gods she had given herself over to were faithless and deceptive.

"My priests and my elders perished in the city / while they sought food to restore their strength themselves"
Even the religious leadership—"my priests and my elders"—proved to be self-serving and under the same condemnation (see Jeremiah 10:21; 14:15–16; Lamentations 2:20; 4:7–9; 5:12). When Nebuchadnezzar cut off the food supplies to Jerusalem, attacking the city for eighteen months, there was a great famine. So great was this famine that mothers boiled their infants and ate them (2:20; 4:10).

VERSE 20

"See, O LORD, for I am in distress"
For a third time, personified Jerusalem calls for the merciful gaze of Yahweh. The word *distress* speaks of "narrow straights." Again, *the only hope to be found in the wake of sin and its distressing consequences is in Yahweh's mercy and grace.* Thus she cries, "See, O LORD." He sees her suffering and has compassion upon her. Hagar found great comfort in this truth after she fled from the

bitter words of Sarai, who despised her. In her pain, Hagar cried out to God, "You are a God who sees" (Genesis 16:13). What did she mean? She rightly concluded: "You are a God who sees me in my affliction. You see me in my need."

"My spirit is greatly troubled; my heart is overturned within me"

This literally reads: "My bowels churn; my heart is overturned inward." The NET Bible reads: "My stomach is in knots! My heart is pounding inside me." The ESV: "My stomach churns; my heart is wrung within me." The reason for the sickness is seen in the next phrase.

"For I have been very rebellious"

This could be translated, "For disobeying I disobeyed." This is a clear and emphatic confession of sin: "For I have been utterly defiant."[14] The suffering God brought on Judah accomplished its purpose—that she realize her sinful ways and repent so that when the people returned from seventy years of captivity in Babylon, they would never return to idolatry.

"In the street the sword slays; in the house it is like death"

Inside or out, there was no escape from the consequences of her sin (see Deuteronomy 32:25). She knew it. She confessed it. She was seeking to embrace it.

Next, personified Jerusalem expresses a measure of faith in God's faithfulness—even if it might be mixed with the bitterness of her pain.

VERSE 21

"They have heard that I groan; there is no one to comfort me; all my enemies have heard of my calamity"

The subject of "no comfort" again surfaces within the prayer-song. The "enemies have heard"—the implication being that they took pleasure in her pain and "calamity." Thus she took the folly of her enemies to the LORD.

---

14 Mackay, 72.

"They are glad that You have done it"

The Hebrew is difficult here. It may be best to understand the phrase "they are glad" as belonging to the preceding thought: "All my enemies have heard of my calamity. They are glad."[15] The final phrase is more literally translated, "When You Yourself have done this." Those hostile to Judah exulted in the distress of Jerusalem's destruction, but they did not understand that Yahweh Himself was behind it. Unbelievers often rejoice in the downfall of God's people, mistakenly assuming that God has failed them or that He is not real—but the remnant of Jerusalem knew that Yahweh Himself had done it. This calamity was not because Yahweh was weak or had failed to help His people. Rather it was from His hand.

The enemy might accuse Israel's God of faithlessness and impotence, but the remnant now knew differently—and thus, in the rest of verses 21 and 22, Jerusalem prayed for the faithfulness of God.

"Oh, that You would bring the day which You have proclaimed, that they may become like me"

This is a plea for God to judge the enemies of Jerusalem as He has judged her. Jeremiah is correct to conclude that God judged Judah and was righteous to do so, but God will also judge Babylon for the sins that she as a nation has committed. God did not choose Babylon as His tool of discipline because she was more righteous than Judah. Judgment was sure to come upon Babylon as well, and when it did, it would be just. In pondering God's righteousness and the words of His mouth that she had disobeyed—in the midst of confession and repentance—Jerusalem remembers the promises of God's Word (see for example Psalm 137:7–9; Isaiah 51:22–23; Jeremiah 48:27ff; 50:11ff; 51:24; Ezekiel 25:2–26:2; Obadiah 12–13; Micah 7:9–10).

VERSE 22

"Let all their wickedness come before You"

See Jeremiah 10:25 (cf. Nehemiah 4:4–5). This is not solely an Old Testament concept (see Revelation 6:10).

---

15 Mackay, 73.

"And deal with them as You have dealt with me / for all my transgressions"
The Lord has dealt with her in righteousness, justice, discipline, and mercy (cf.
1:12–18). See 2 Thessalonians 1:6–10 for a New Testament parallel. Walter Kaiser explains the manner in which the New Testament teaching on loving one's
enemies relates to this:

> But what about this prayer that the Lord would do to Jerusalem's enemies
> as they had done to her? Must the Christian blush and set aside this teaching in favour of Christ's word in Matthew 5:44, "Love your enemies?"
>
> Such a strong contrast between the testaments is unfair. For one
> thing, the injunction of our Lord in Matthew 5:44 came from the Old
> Testament (Exodus 23:4–5; Leviticus 19:18; Proverbs 25:21–22; cf.
> Rom. 12:20). Love for one's enemy was not an optional luxury in either
> testament.[16]

But there was another matter:

> There are two kinds of enemies. Some who bear ill-will towards us personally for private reasons (which) concern ourselves alone. When the
> matter extends no further than to our own person, then we should
> privately commend it to God, and pray for those who are ill-disposed
> towards us…to do them good, and not return evil for evil, but rather
> overcome evil with good (Romans 12:17, 21). But if our enemies are
> of that sort, that they bear ill-will toward us, not for any private cause,
> but on account of matters of faith; and are also opposed not only to us,
> but especially to God in Heaven…; then indeed we should pray that
> God would convert those who may be converted, but as for those who
> continue ever to rage, stubbornly and maliciously, against God and His
> Church, that God would execute upon them according to His own
> sentence, judgment and righteousness (Psalm 139:19).[17]

---

16 Kaiser, 57.

17 Cramer, as cited by C.W. Eduard Nagelsbach, *The Lamentations of Jeremiah*, trans., enlarged, and
   ed. William H. Hornblower in Lange's *Commentary on the Holy Scriptures*, 25 vols. (New York:
   Scribner, Armstrong, 1870), 3:67—quoted by Kaiser, 58.

"For my groans are many and my heart is faint"

The first song ends with a confession that though Yahweh is righteous, just, and faithful, the pain is still very real. This could be translated, "For my sighs/gasps are many and my heart is sick." Jerusalem thus confesses her weak and weary state.

INSIGHTS FOR COUNSELING

As it was in Jeremiah's day, so it is in ours. When we respond properly to the sorrow our sin has caused, it produces a deep repentance that leads to a firm commitment to please God from that day forward. Unfortunately, many people suffer greatly under great sorrow but never get to this point. Instead, they remain sad and bitter about all they've lost, filled with grief over the destruction in their life, their marriage, or their family, but they fail to reach the point of admitting, "This is *my* doing. This is *my* fault. God is chastening *me*. It is *I* who have brought this misery into my life." As a result, God's mercy seems to elude them. As miserable as the realization of our sin is, it is a necessary step to our being restored to God. Without a full acknowledgment of the depth of our sin against Him, any remedy God offers us will seem cheap. True hope is born out of deep repentance.

This type of confession and repentance—faith, hope, and prayer—is not a recipe to make the temporal consequences of sin go away, but it is the path to recovery, faith, and a restored joy and testimony. Immeasurable comfort can be found in the glorious gospel truth that the sinless Messiah suffered the infinite and eternal consequences of sin as our substitute (Isaiah 53; 2 Corinthians 5:21; 1 Peter 2:24–25)!

Many sufferers have been encouraged by the Word of God recorded in the first chapter of Lamentations. We learn that we must not run *from* God in shame because of sin's misery, but rather run *to* Him with our misery if we desire His mercy. In light of this, we must take time to consider numerous biblical principles.

1. Before mercy can be experienced, one's misery must be understood from a divine perspective.

There must be humble repentance that confesses one simple reality: "God is righteous to destroy me because of my sin. Therefore, I do not deserve His mercy." Only then can there truly be a new beginning. It is crucial to note that the cause of the prophet's misery on behalf of Judah is not chiefly the devastation he witnesses, though that certainly has made him miserable. The root cause of the pain is his full realization that Judah herself is to blame. *Her* deep-seated rebellion against God's Word and *her* pride and stubbornness caused her ruin. All blame shifting is finally gone; this is true brokenness (Lamentations 1:12, 14; Proverbs 16:18; Psalm 51:17).

2. When faced with the grievous consequences of sin, it is appropriate to chronicle our pain, loneliness, and despair and recount from where we have fallen.

Though we must not sinfully *dwell* on the past or the consequences of sin alone, it is appropriate to honestly face the devastating losses experienced because of sin, as well as our current state of humiliation (Lamentations 1:1–11a; Philippians 3:13–14; Psalm 51:3).

3. Friendship with the world is hostility toward God—and in the end, the world will be an unfaithful lover who betrays us.

Our idols will fail to satisfy and will ultimately forsake us. Like Judah, we too often turn to worldly solutions—only to be left bereft of any lasting hope, satisfaction, or true joy (Lamentations 1:2, 19; James 4:4; 1 John 2:15–16).

4. We can recite our losses and acknowledge quite bluntly our pain, but in the midst of this we must remember 1) the sovereignty of the true God of the Bible and 2) the "ultimate cause" of all suffering—sin and rebellion against God.

The personal value of any suffering is lost when we don't humbly submit to God's sovereign will. This is true of suffering we bring upon ourselves, as in the case of Judah, as well as suffering we experience in the wake of the sins of others, as in the case of Jeremiah. When we identify sin as the "ultimate cause" of all suffering, we are not saying that all personal suffering is the result of one's own personal sin. However, we do need to recognize that there was no suffering prior to man's fall into sin in Genesis 3, and therefore, the "ultimate cause" of all suffering is sin and rebellion. Since we have each inherited our sin nature from

Adam, we must each acknowledge that there exists no good thing in our flesh and consequently bow our will to the will of the sovereign Lord who appoints our pain. Only when we submit to our suffering will we recognize its true value (Lamentations 1:18; Psalm 103:19; Romans 7:18).

5. One of the greatest sources of pain and aloneness experienced by a penitent believer is that of the loss of testimony.

A *testimony* is a believer's Christian reputation before a watching world. Our witness, or testimony, concerning God's righteousness is often mocked and ridiculed as hypocritical and worthless when the world around us sees sin's consequences in our lives (Lamentations 1:7–9a; Philippians 2:14–16; Titus 2:5).

6. We must remember that sin leads to dishonor and shame.

Sin delivers only part of what it promises. It promises fleshly pleasure, as well as freedom from the confines of God's laws. However, the pleasure it supplies is only temporary, while the so-called freedom from God's authority often results in long-lasting enslavement to sin and to the devil (Lamentations 1:16–17; Romans 6:16; James 1:13–15).

7. It is always appropriate to cry out to God for mercy.

Therein lies the hope of every believer, faint as it may be at times. Don't be stubborn. Don't be proud. Don't be like Judah and stiffen your neck against God. What use is that? What good will that bring you? Isaiah writes, "Seek the LORD while He may be found, call upon Him while He is near" (55:6; cf. Lamentations 1:20).

8. Many times we feel that no one understands what we are going through.

We must wage war against these self-centered thoughts by recalling the unimaginable depth of humility borne by the Lord Jesus in His incarnation, especially the depth of grief and pain He endured for us at Calvary. There is no pain like the pain He suffered for our sins. Even so, we cannot engage in comparisons of our levels of suffering. This is a vanity and distraction from what God intends to teach us in our trial (Lamentations 1:1–2; Isaiah 53:4; Mark 15:34; 1 Corinthians 10:13; Hebrews 4:15).

9. When we lose sight of the fact that there are consequences to sin (consequences we do not see now but will see in the days ahead), our natural tendency is to sin without limit.

We must keep in mind the holiness of God and the future day in which He will judge sin. Like Moses, we must also train ourselves to look to the joy of eternal reward that always surpasses the temporal pleasure of sin. Unlike Judah, we must deliberately consider our future (Lamentations 1:8, 12–15; Hebrews 11:24–26).

10. The grief caused by our sin becomes a gift when it brings us to the realization of how deeply we have transgressed against God and, therefore, makes us ready to receive His mercy and grace.

By God's grace, we are able to conclude that for too long we have been tolerant of our sin and complacent in our pursuit of holiness. Things must change in our lives, or all hope will be lost forever. That is the verdict Jeremiah comes to in Lamentations. In like manner, we must personally recognize our guilt before God and be willing to face it honestly (Lamentations 1:15–18; Luke 13:1–5; Hebrews 3:15; 4:7; Revelation 2:5).

11. Not only is God ultimately sovereign over our suffering, but He also intervenes as the comforter in our sorrows.

He is "the Father of mercies and God of all comfort, who comforts us in all our affliction" (2 Corinthians 1:3–4). Many say or imply that it is awfully cruel for a sovereign God to create misery and then fly to the rescue as our comforter. But that is not the right picture. The misery is *our* responsibility; it is because of *our* sin. We *should* be miserable. However, in our misery we must quickly run to God for mercy lest we become trapped in a dark cave of despair so filled with self-worship that we become totally blinded to the grace of God (Lamentations 1:20; James 4:8–10).

12. At the end of your discipline, you can only say, "It is good for me," if you have learned what God sought to teach you.

The psalmist confesses, "It is good for me that I was afflicted, that I may learn Your statutes" (Psalm 119:71). The author of Hebrews explains, "Now no chastening seems to be joyful for the present, but painful; nevertheless, afterward it yields the peaceable fruit of righteousness *to those who have been trained by it*" (Hebrews 12:11). Only after Job was humbled by his affliction (which was not caused by personal sin, but was still overwhelmingly painful) was he able to testify: "I have heard of Thee by the hearing of the ear; but now my eye sees Thee" (42:5). When you have "seen" God in a new way (have understood His character and learned to trust His ways) as a result of your suffering, He becomes more precious to you than ever before, and your heart is filled with thanksgiving, realizing, "It is His kindness that leads us to repentance" (Romans 2:4). When Jeremiah admitted, on behalf of his nation, "For I have been very rebellious," though outward circumstances did not change for the better, spiritual profit began to be received internally (Lamentations 1:18, 20).

13. God fashions the consequences of our sin for maximum effectiveness.

Jeremiah describes the effects of Judah's sin: "The yoke of my transgressions is bound; by His hand they are knit together" (Lamentations 1:14). Because God loves us and wants us to walk with Him in true faith and holiness, He brings us to the point where we are broken. Many who refuse to let go of their sin and come to Christ for cleansing have not been brought low enough, even though from the perspective of an outsider it might appear they could not go any lower. To think rightly about our sin means we must admit our guilt to the Lord and humbly accept the consequences that our sin has brought into our lives. Only then are we prepared to receive the grace of forgiveness (Lamentations 1:9b–10; Luke 8:43–48; Psalm 51:17).

14. In the wake of the suffering that sin causes, we cannot carelessly "move on with life," knowing that we have tromped on the holiness of God by rebelliously going our own way.

We must see how serious sin is before God. He will not let us continually say to Him, "I have no use for You. You have no part in my life. I'll come to You on occasion—when I am super desperate—but otherwise leave me alone!" God will not tolerate that attitude. For the mercy of God to be fully realized, we must stop to take notice of our rebellion and honestly repent before Him, trusting in the shed blood of Christ alone as the basis for our reconciliation with God (Lamentations 1:18, 20; Isaiah 53:6; 2 Corinthians 5:21; 1 Peter 3:18).

Homework for Counseling

You are encouraged to photocopy homework pages for use in personal counseling.

Part 1: Thinking Rightly About Sin

Before we can be assured of God's mercy, we need to begin to think rightly about our sin. As described in the first chapter of Lamentations, Jeremiah and the people could not receive the mercy of God until they had come to three realizations concerning sin.

1. Our sin provokes God's anger, and He brings about painful consequences.

"Look and see if there is any pain like my pain, which was severely dealt out to me, which the Lord inflicted on the day of His fierce anger" (Lamentations 1:12).

- Read Lamentations 1:1–11a, and consider some of the consequences of Judah's sin. List the many forms of humiliation and suffering that are part of your current situation. (Note: your list will not be limited to, or necessarily include, the same painful suffering Judah experienced)
- Place an *X* next to the ones in your list that you think are consequences of your own sinful choices.
- When and where (at what place in your life) did you turn onto the path of sin? What did that path look like? Did anyone seek to persuade you to change your ways?
- Read Psalm 51:1–4. Before David could be fully cleansed of the guilt of his adulterous encounter with Bathsheba, he had to come to an important realization. What did David realize in verse 4? Have you come to the same realization about your sin?

2. Our sin often affects us physically, sapping us of strength and stamina.

"From on high He sent fire into my bones, and it prevailed over them.... [I am] faint all day long.... He has made my strength fail" (Lamentations 1:13–15)

- Do you believe you are facing any physical effects from your sin, such as a lack of energy and vitality (cf. Lam. 1:13-15)? What are you experiencing?

- Read Psalm 38. What were some of the physical effects of David's sin? What was his only hope for relief?

3. Our sin often causes us to experience shame in ourselves and before others, and therefore, we must assume personal responsibility for it.

"For these things I weep.... My children are desolate because the enemy has prevailed. Zion stretches out her hands; there is no one to comfort her...Jerusalem has become an unclean thing among them" (Lamentations 1:16–17).

- Do you feel it is ever appropriate to be ashamed? For what reason?
- Read Genesis 3:1–10. What was it that caused Adam and Eve to feel shame?
- Read Hebrews 12:1–3. How did Jesus take our shame?

Part 2: Thinking Rightly About God

Before we can be assured of God's mercy, we must also begin to think rightly about our God. If our plea for mercy is to be heard by Him, we must think correctly about the One to whom we cry out. In Lamentations 1, Jeremiah came to four important conclusions about God.

1. God is right to discipline His children.

"The Lord is righteous; for I have rebelled against His command" (Lamentations 1:18).

- Do you believe that God is too loving, too gracious, or too merciful to inflict pain on you as a consequence for your sin? Why or why not?
- Proverbs 3:11 says, "My son, do not reject the discipline of the LORD or loathe His reproof." In other words, we must not openly reject God's discipline or quietly chafe under it. Why do you think this is?
- Read Proverbs 3:12. Why does the Bible say we must not complain about God's discipline? Can you think of any reason to complain about it?
- Read Hebrews 12:5–11. Why does God discipline His children? What is the proper response to divine discipline? Are you responding biblically to your present discipline from God? Do you believe that God has custom-designed your suffering as a form of discipline to train you in righteousness?

- Consider the following quote: "No truth is more affecting than
  that God still loves and suffers with those whom He is obliged in
  righteousness to smite."[18] Does this truth "affect" you? That is, does it
  help you understand that God is right to discipline you?
- Why must we rightly conclude that divine discipline is a mark of God's
  love for us?
- Perhaps you need to say to God, "Thank You for loving me enough
  to spank me. Forgive me for being bitter and angry at You. What
  right do I have to ever be angry at You? Forgive me, Lord. Teach me
  to submit to Your discipline so that I will be trained to follow in Your
  righteousness."
- Write out a prayer of thanks to God for loving you enough to discipline
  you. If necessary, ask God's forgiveness for being angry with Him and
  for whatever sinful attitudes you have had regarding your discipline.

2. God is the only One who can truly satisfy us.

"I have called to my lovers, but they have deceived me" (Lamentations 1:19).

- When the people of Judah found themselves in dire straits, they
  declared in effect, "I called to my idols, my false gods, all the things
  I have placed my hope in and chosen to worship. But in my time of
  greatest need, they were not there for me."
- Are you in a time of great need in your life? What are some of the
  things that you have been absorbed by in place of God (cf. 1:19)? List
  as many as you can. How have they let you down?
- Suffering often has a way of stripping us of the useless, time-wasting
  distractions we fill our lives with and the golden calves we craft for our
  own pleasure. Suffering scrapes away these idols, leaving us wanting
  only God.
- Read Psalm 73:25–26. Is God the strength of your heart? Is He your
  portion forever? Are you ultimately satisfied with Him? If you think
  you are, then why do you keep pursuing so many other false gods,
  other means of satisfaction?

---

18 J. Sidlow Baxter, *Explore the Book*, vol. 6 (Grand Rapids: Zondervan, 1960), 286.

• Read Colossians 3:1–4. Write out your thoughts on what your life might look like if you were preoccupied with Christ and His cross.

3. God sees us in our distress.

"See, O LORD, for I am in distress; my spirit is greatly troubled; my heart is over-turned within me, for I have been very rebellious" (Lamentations 1:20).

• Do you believe that God truly sees your affliction and desires to come to your aid?

• Sometimes, when we are treading the deep waters of suffering, Satan tempts us to think that God is nowhere to be found. But the truth is that God sees even the minutest detail of our situation and is there to help and give comfort. In light of Lamentations 1:11b, 18–20, write out your own prayer to the Lord, confessing any sin and idolatry and seeking His mercy and forgiveness.

4. God will judge all sin righteously.

"Let all their wickedness come before You; and deal with them as You have dealt with me for all my transgressions" (Lamentations 1:22).

• Are you confident that God will take care of punishing sin? Are you ever frustrated when others appear to "get away with their sin" (cf. 1:22)? What are some examples in your experience?

• In light of Genesis 12:3, how might Judah's prayer in Lamentations 1:22 differ from an individual's request? Yet it is appropriate to pray that God's justice will bring about repentance in others who have sinned. Why?

• Read Romans 12:17–21. Sometimes our suffering comes at the hands of others. Is God still in control? What is our responsibility according to this Scripture?

• How does your thinking need to change about sin and about God? Pray Psalm 51 back to God, confessing specific sins as needed and asking God to turn your heart toward His Word.

PART 3: HOPING IN JESUS

So where does all of this thinking about our sin and God's righteousness bring us? It directs us to the only true source of hope—Jesus. There is no hope anywhere else. No hope in our solving our own problems, cleaning up our own lives, or making up for the sins we have committed. Hope is found only in humbling ourselves before the One who says, "Come to Me, all who are weary and heavy-laden, and I will give you rest. Take My yoke upon you and learn from Me, for I am gentle and humble in heart, and you will find rest for your souls. For My yoke is easy and My burden is light" (Matthew 11:28–30).

This may mean you need to come to the end of yourself for the very first time, to let the painful consequences of sin do the work God has sent them to accomplish. For the first time in your life, you must reach out with empty hands of faith to Jesus, who said, "Come to Me. Come to Me, and I will forgive you. Come to Me, and I will cleanse you. Come to Me, and I will give you rest in the midst of your pain and affliction."

Come to Jesus and He will accept you. Not because you are acceptable, but because *He* has already been accepted by God and gives that same acceptance to those who repent and believe in Him. He lives now to save you from your sin and bring you back to God.

- Read Hebrews 7:23–27. What is the basis of any sinner's acceptance with God? What does the Bible mean when it refers to Jesus as the Great High Priest for sinners? What does it mean that Jesus lives to intercede for sinners?
- If you have been a believer in Christ for quite some time, this is another opportunity to come to Him. It is a time to thank Him for absorbing the wrath of God against your sins so that you don't have to endure it for all of eternity.
- Read Romans 5:6–10. What kind of people did Jesus die for? What is the greatest demonstration of the love of God?
- Write out your own prayer of thanks to God for Jesus and for His cross of reconciliation.

Chapter 2

"POUR OUT YOUR HEART LIKE WATER"

A Song of Sovereignty and Divine Discipline

Lamentations 2:1–22

As the prophet writes this second song lamenting the destruction of Jerusalem, he wants us to understand clearly from the beginning that God is the One who has done this. As the people of God look at the city—once beautiful and well populated, now destroyed and empty—the prophet wants them to know: "God has done this to you."

In the first ten verses, forty references point to God's judgment and anger.[1] Forty times in ten verses! Jeremiah does not want us to miss the point. We must make no mistake about it. We must put away from our minds any fragment of a perverted theology that refuses to give God credit for suffering since God in His Word identifies Himself as its sovereign cause. Of course, He does not take credit for the sin that serves as the instrumental cause. God is holy. We are responsible for our sin. But in His providential work in human history, God takes credit for the suffering and affliction we find ourselves in.

---

1 Walter C. Kaiser, Jr., *Grief and Pain in the Plan of God* (Fearn: Christian Focus, 2004), 59.

Isaiah 45:7 says, "The One forming light and creating darkness, causing well-being and creating calamity; I am the LORD who does all these." If God is not ultimately in control of both what we consider to be "good" and "calamity," then any real hope for humans is destroyed. If evil, or Satan himself, is free to steal, kill, and destroy without God's permission, then there is nowhere for man to turn for help.

Though all pain and suffering is the result of the curse of sin upon earth and some personal suffering is the result of personal sin, the Bible consistently identifies *God* as the One who ultimately orders our afflictions. Whether our suffering is a direct consequence of our own sin, or the sins of others, the truth remains that the pain is meant to purify us and bring us back to God in a humble spirit of repentance.

If we are going to let suffering accomplish its deep work of sanctification in our hearts, then we must deal with the pain birthed by sin, which God uses to get our attention. Just as physical pain signals something wrong in the body, the pain of suffering alerts us to the presence of poison in our spiritual bloodstream. Pain, especially pain that comes from the chastening hand of God, is therefore beneficial to us. "All discipline for the moment seems not to be joyful, but sorrowful," says the writer of Hebrews, "yet to those who have been trained by it, afterwards it yields the peaceful fruit of righteousness" (Hebrews 12:11).

God's holiness and justice forbid Him from looking the other way when His people sin. He loves us too much to let us remain content with our sinful ways. He is long-suffering and kind, but at the same time He is a God who judges sin and, therefore, will discipline His own when they go astray in order to prevent their condemnation. However, we must submit to His discipline in order to fully profit from it. How do we do this? Lamentations 2 answers that question.

In Lamentations 2 we will see three movements that will help us process and deal with the severe discipline of the Lord in our lives, and perhaps others' as well.

TEACHING OUTLINES

Option A

I. A song of sorrow and despair (1:1–22)
II. A song of sovereignty and divine discipline (2:1–22)
   A. The discipline of the sovereign Lord recounted (2:1–10)
      1. The Lord's destruction of Israel's worldly pride (2:1–5)
         a. He has cast from heaven to earth, the glory of Israel (v. 1)
         b. He has thrown down, the strongholds of the daughter of Judah (v. 2)
         c. He has cut off all the strength of Israel (v. 3)
         d. He has poured out His wrath like fire (v. 4)
         e. He has destroyed her strongholds (v. 5)
      2. The Lord's destruction of Israel's religious pride (2:6–10)
         a. He has violently treated His tabernacle (v. 6)
         b. He has rejected His altar (v. 7)
         c. He has destroyed Israel's confidence (vv. 8–10)
            i. The wall (v. 8)
            ii. The gates (v. 9a)
            iii. The political leadership (v. 9b)
            iv. The religious leadership (v. 9c)
            v. The mourning of society (v. 10)
   B. The discipleship of the songwriter recorded (2:11–19)
      1. Compassion concerning the pain (2:11–12)
         a. The compassionate sorrow expressed (v. 11)
         b. The cruel suffering illustrated (v. 12)
      2. Clarity and realism concerning sin and its consequences (2:13–17)
         a. You have been damaged beyond measure (v. 13)
         b. You have been deceived by false prophets (v. 14)
         c. You have been degraded by all and the truth is mocked (v. 15)
         d. You have been despised by your enemies (v. 16)
         e. You have been delivered up by Yahweh in faithfulness to His Word [thus there is an implicit hope concerning Yahweh's promises of restoration] (v. 17)

    3. Counsel concerning devastation and faith (2:18–19)

        a. Pursue the Lord incessantly in your grief (v. 18)

        b. Pour out your heart to the Lord in prayer and petition (v. 19)

C. The devastation and flickering faith of the suffering city recited before the LORD (2:20–22)

    1. The petition of faith, seeking mercy (v. 20a)

    2. The prayer of devastation, seeking mercy (vv. 20b–22)

        a. Questions that reveal the horror, yet imply faith in the righteousness of God (v. 20b)

        b. Confirmation of the Lord's righteous judgment, which implies that the only hope is His mercy (vv. 21–22)

           i. In the day of Your anger (v. 21)

          ii. In the day of the LORD's anger (v. 22)

Option B

I. Jeremiah recognized God's anger as being righteous (vv. 1–10)

    A. God removed Judah's glory (v. 1)

    B. God humbled the people (v. 2)

    C. God withheld His protection (v. 3)

    D. God treated Judah as an enemy (vv. 4–5)

    E. God discarded His temple and punished the priests (vv. 6–7)

    F. God destroyed the city wall and its gates (vv. 8–9)

    G. God caused much grief (v. 10)

II. Jeremiah realized the grief and suffering that sin brings on others (vv. 11–12)

III. Jeremiah regretted sin and its painful consequences (vv. 13–17)

    A. Sin devastates (v. 13)

    B. Sin deceives (v. 14)

    C. Sin degrades (vv. 15–16)

    D. Sin delivers (v. 17)

IV. Jeremiah requested mercy from God (vv. 18–22)

    A. Their grief drove them to the compassion of God (vv. 18–19)

    B. Their hope rested in the faithfulness of God (v. 20)

    C. Their faith looked to the mercy of God (vv. 21–22)

EXPOSITION
VERSE 1

How the Lord has covered the daughter of Zion / with a cloud
in His anger!

Again this chapter begins with an exclamatory cry: "How" ("Alas," "Ah" [cf. 1:1; 4:1]). "Ah, *Adonai* [the sovereign Master] has overshadowed with anger, the daughter of Zion" (author's translation). At one time, Jerusalem had been the resting place of God's glory cloud as it filled the temple (see 1 Kings 8:10–11). Now, however, Jeremiah sings a lament about God's anger cloud enveloping "the daughter of Zion."

He has cast from heaven to earth / the glory of Israel

The word translated *glory* here can also be rendered *beauty*. Israel's beauty was once exalted to heaven as God's glory cloud rested in the temple, but now a divine cloud of wrath has enveloped the city. As a result of God's anger toward Judah's sin, He has cast her from heaven to earth and has removed her glory. Perhaps, as Guest remarks: "The poet was haunted by the memory of a cloud of smoke enveloping Jerusalem, filling his lungs with the stench of burning walls and of burning flesh." The glorious city is now a pile of smoking ruins.

And has not remembered His footstool / in the day of His anger

The word *remember* speaks of more than just mental recollection, but rather of care and protection. His "footstool" is a reference to the Ark of the Covenant, particularly the mercy seat where God sat in judgment over sin. He has not remembered His mercy. The Sovereign Master has said, "I have had it with these rebellious people!" As Kaiser notes:

> "The splendour of Israel" was her Temple (Isaiah 64:11; see also 60:7; 63:15) and her "ark of the covenant" (Psalm 78:60–61; cf. 1 Samuel 4:21–22). Likewise, God's "footstool" was identified in 1 Chronicles 28:2 with the ark [Jeremiah 3:16 would occur later; cf. 2 Chronicles 35:3]. David said there: "I had in mine heart to build a house of rest for the ark of covenant of the Lord; that is for the footstool of our

God." The reason the ark was named His footstool is that the Lord was enthroned and seated between the cherubim (1 Samuel 4:4; 2 Samuel 6:2; Psalm 80:1; 99:1, 5; 132:7), which were over the ark of the covenant; thus the Lord's feet rested on the cover of the ark (mercy seat) and He spoke "from above the mercy seat" (Exodus 25:22; Numbers 7:89). So great then was the wrath and anger of God at the depth of Judah's sin that He even abandoned His footstool in the day of His anger.[2]

The "day of [God's] anger" will be cited again in verse 22, to form brackets around this second poem. The reference to the Lord's "anger" or "displeasure" is repeated in 2:3, 6, 21, 22. Divine anger is not some irrational emotion, but rather a "sign that the universe is not ultimately irrational, but moral, guided and accountable."[3]

VERSE 2

The LORD has swallowed up; He has not spared / all the habitations of Jacob

Again, *Adonai* is acknowledged as the One who has severely humbled Israel. The poet laments that God's anger has essentially eaten Israel alive. Concerning the prophet's description of the holy city, Charles Dyer writes, "The words Jeremiah used depict an image of God personally overseeing the dismantling of the city. [The Hebrew verb meaning] 'to swallow up' or 'to engulf completely' was used four times...perhaps to picture the fire of God's judgment engulfing the city itself... God was the 'one-man wrecking crew' responsible for the rubble."[4] "Habitations of Jacob" speak of the dwelling places or homes in Israel. The NET Bible reads: "The Lord destroyed mercilessly all the homes of Jacob's descendants."

In His wrath He has thrown down / the strongholds of the daughter of Judah

"In His fury/wrath He has broken down the fortifications of the daughter of Judah" (author's translation). Observers might have protested that it was the

---

2 Kaiser, 66.

3 John L. Mackay, *Lamentations: A Mentor Commentary* (Fearn: Christian Focus, 2008), 95.

4 Charles H. Dyer in Roy B. Zuck and John F. Walvoord, eds. *The Bible Knowledge Commentary* (Wheaton: Victor Books, 1985), 1214.

Babylonians who had "thrown down the strongholds of the daughter of Judah," but Jeremiah records that it was God's sovereign work.

He has brought them down to the ground; He has profaned the kingdom and its princes

The NET Bible reads: "He knocked to the ground and humiliated the kingdom and its rulers." The idea is of profaning something held sacred—the destruction of an idol. "The sovereign Master struck them to the ground; He has polluted the kingdom and its princes" (author's translation). Israel's society had become a filthy idol that God cut down and humiliated so that all could see that it had no intrinsic glory in itself. It is God who lowered them. Jeremiah had been informed of this judgment ahead of time, when he was first called by God: "See, I have appointed you this day over the nations and over the kingdoms, to pluck up and to break down, to destroy and to overthrow, to build and to plant" (Jeremiah 1:10).

VERSE 3

In fierce anger He has cut off / all the strength of Israel

The word *strength* here is literally *horn*. In 2 Chronicles 34:4, 7, the verb *cut off* is translated, "chopped down." The "strength" of Israel was an idol that the Sovereign Lord chopped down in "burning anger."

He has drawn back His right hand / from before the enemy

The "right hand" represented the hand of position and power. Again, the Sovereign One had withdrawn His power and protection and allowed "the enemy" to overpower Israel. Notably, Babylon is not explicitly mentioned as Israel's enemy. Rather the focus is on the sovereign judgment and discipline of the Lord in withholding the protection He had once provided.

And He has burned Jacob like a flaming fire / consuming round about

The Lord's wrath is here pictured as a "flaming fire" that "devours all around." It was "Jacob/Israel" whom "He has burned." See Deuteronomy 4:24–28 for God's character as a consuming fire and jealous God in the context of a warning against idolatry.

Verse 4

He has bent His bow like an enemy; He has set His right hand like an adversary

Here Jeremiah states explicitly what was implied in the previous verse. The Sovereign Lord treated His own chosen people like an enemy. It was "*His* bow" that was behind the Chaldeans' weapons. God's "right hand" not only allowed the enemy access to Israel and Jerusalem (v. 3), but His sovereign and all-powerful "hand" was set "like an adversary." In previous days, Yahweh's right hand had been a source of comfort, joy, and deliverance (Exodus 15:6, 12). Now it was like an adversary.

And slain all that were pleasant to the eye

The NLT renders this phrase: "His strength is used against them to kill their finest youth." The NET Bible: "Like a foe he killed everyone, even our strong young men." The NRSV: "He has killed all in whom we took pride." Lamentations 1:18 may shed more light on this expression. Again God is depicted as active in His punishment of the nation.

In the tent of the daughter of Zion / He has poured out His wrath like fire

The "tent of the daughter of Zion" refers to the place where they lived—Jerusalem. The city had become an object of divine "wrath" that God "poured out... like fire." This seems to emphasize what was stated in verse 3. The prophet Amos promised this in Amos 2:4–5: "Thus says the LORD, 'For three transgressions of Judah and for four I will not revoke its punishment; because they rejected the law of the LORD and have not kept His statues; their lies also have led them astray, those after which their fathers walked. *So I will send fire upon Judah and it will consume the citadels of Jerusalem.*'"

Verse 5

The Lord has become like an enemy

Note again the phrase "as an enemy" (v. 4; see also v. 3). The Sovereign Master had become hostile toward His covenant nation. Perhaps the preposition *like* implies fledgling faith that understands that God is not an *actual* enemy, but in His wisdom He has acted "like an enemy" for their ultimate good. God treated His people like He had treated the other nations. What a horrible thought! Yet God warned them of this. In both Leviticus and Deuteronomy, Moses warned the people of God's judgment upon their disobedience, in effect saying, "If you disobey Me then I will chasten you. I will turn you out. I will judge you."

He has swallowed up Israel; He has swallowed up all its palaces, He has destroyed its strongholds

"Swallowed up" or "devoured" was used in 2:2, twice here in verse 5, and in 2:8, 16 as well. It is used elsewhere to describe the actual ground opening up and devouring those under judgment. It speaks of God's holy, consuming, and devouring punishment upon those who oppose Him (see Psalm 21:8–9).

"Strongholds" were also mentioned in verse 2. See also Psalm 89:38–46 for a parallel portion of a song dealing with God's humiliation of Israel's pride.

And multiplied in the daughter of Judah / mourning and moaning

The phrase "mourning and moaning" is an attempt in English to echo the poetic flair of the Hebrew here. "Sorrow and sadness" or "weeping and wailing" might also work.

The main point of verses 1–5 is that God—as Sovereign Master—has destroyed Israel's worldly pride and thus the objects to their looking to insure their success. He cast from heaven to earth (v. 1); He profaned the kingdom and its princes (v. 2); He cut off all the strength of Israel (v. 3); He killed all those pleasant to the eye (v. 4); and He swallowed up all its palaces and destroyed its strongholds (v. 5). But God's sovereign chastening did not stop there.

VERSE 6

And He has violently treated His tabernacle like a garden booth

Like a farmer who erects a temporary shelter in the field only to demolish and discard it after he is done with fieldwork, so Israel's Sovereign Master treated "His tabernacle," the temple (cf. *Constable's Expository Notes on the Bible*; see also Jeremiah 7:4, 8–15).

He has destroyed His appointed meeting place

Israel's religious and social life centered on Jerusalem, specifically the temple. But now Jeremiah sings of the destruction of that "appointed meeting place."

The LORD has caused to be forgotten / the appointed feast
and Sabbath in Zion

As a result of the destruction of the temple, "the appointed feast and Sabbath in Zion" were "forgotten." Incredibly, Yahweh Himself "caused" it (see 1:15).

And He has despised king and priest / in the indignation of His anger

Yahweh had made a covenant with David concerning both "king" and the "house" of God in 2 Samuel 7:12–19, which would in turn house the "priest[s]." In the destruction of the temple, Jeremiah saw both "king and priest" rejected "in the indignation of His anger." Though certainly Jeremiah understood in some measure the enduring promises of the Davidic covenant and even the hope of the New Covenant, he still lamented the divine denunciation of king and priest in the destruction of the temple. Not even the leaders escaped God's judgment (again see Psalm 89:40).

VERSE 7

The Lord has rejected His altar, He has abandoned His sanctuary

The altar that was intended to bring a "soothing aroma" (Exodus 29:41), *Adonai* had "rejected." He had also "abandoned His sanctuary." See Ezekiel 10 and the vision of God's glory departing from the temple.

He has delivered into the hand of the enemy / the walls of her palaces

It was Israel's Sovereign Master who had shut the enemy's hand over "the walls of her palaces."

They have made a noise in the house of the LORD / as in the day
of an appointed feast

Instead of Israel celebrating "in the house of Yahweh," it was her enemy making "noise in the house of Yahweh." The heathen enemies, who were not allowed anywhere near the temple, marched in, murdered the priests, destroyed everything in sight, and let loose shouts of triumph, which sounded like shouts of celebration from the people "as in the day of an appointed feast." This was a total reversal. Imagine the grief in God's heart as He destroyed His own temple in His righteous anger, including the altar, where millions of animals had been slaughtered to atone for the sins of His people. What a mockery it was to have pagans crying out in celebration and perhaps pagan worship in the house of the true and living God.

Verse 8

The Lord determined to destroy / the wall of the daughter of Zion
It was Yahweh who had "determined to destroy the wall" in Jerusalem, not Nebuchadnezzar's army (see Jeremiah 52:13–14; 2 Kings 25:9–10).

He has stretched out a line, He has not restrained His hand from destroying
"He has stretched out a line" pictures the Lord as a Builder, but in this context as One who will deconstruct Jerusalem—"destroying" it (cf. 2 Kings 21:13; Isaiah 34:11; Amos 7:7 for similar terminology). Like a surveyor, God went into the city with His measuring line and decided to raze the entire property. Yahweh demolished Jerusalem.

And He has caused rampart and wall to lament; they have languished together
"Rampart and wall" are depicted as mourning. A *rampart* speaks of a fortified wall. Both the fortified walls and the rest of the walls have become weak, "languished." It was Yahweh who caused them to weep and become weak.

Verse 9

Her gates have sunk into the ground, He has destroyed and broken her bars
Jerusalem's "gates" had become part of "the ground." God had "destroyed and broken" Jerusalem's protection.

Her king and her princes are among the nations

A blind and childless Zedekiah (2 Kings 25:7) and Johoiachin and his sons were "among the nations" (24:10–16).

The law is no more; also her prophets find / no vision from the LORD

With the temple gone and the priesthood decimated, "the law" was no more. Yes, Jeremiah, Ezekiel, and Daniel all prophesied after the destruction of Jerusalem, but "her prophets"—those Jerusalem had formerly looked to—found "no vision from Yahweh." See Jeremiah 18:18 for the people's attitude prior to the destruction (cf. also Jeremiah 8). In addition to God destroying the city's defenses and judging her leaders, worst of all, He stopped speaking to them. As a mark of God's judgment, His revelation temporarily ceased.

VERSE 10

The elders of the daughter of Zion / sit on the ground, they are silent

"Elders" refers to those who were elders in age and may speak of those who were leaders in Israel. God brought much grief into their experience, as they too "are silent" and humiliated, sitting "on the ground." No one would honor them or listen anymore.

They have thrown dust on their heads; they have girded themselves with sackcloth

These silenced elders are pictured as mourning, as evidenced by the "dust on their heads" and the "sackcloth." These are all images of great grief and suffering.

The virgins of Jerusalem / have bowed their heads to the ground

"Virgins" may reference those who accompanied the singers in temple worship (1:4). From elder to virgin, Jerusalem is in pain, grief, and mourning. Second Chronicles 36:17 describes this: "Therefore He brought up against them the king of the Chaldeans who slew their young men with the sword in the house of their sanctuary, and had no compassion on young man or virgin, old man or infirm; He gave them all into his hand." There was no preferential treatment, no partiality. God judged, and He judged them all. There was *much* grief.

VERSE 11

My eyes fail because of tears / my spirit is greatly troubled; my heart is poured out on the earth

Incredibly, instead of expressing feelings of vindication and self-righteous superiority after preaching for decades against Israel's sin and idolatry and warning them of the coming judgment, God's messenger, Jeremiah, was deeply affected by Judah's sin. Here he communicates his great compassion and sorrow for his people. He tells the nation that his "eyes are worn out from weeping" (NET). His stomach was in knots (cf. NET), and his liver/bile was poured out on the ground (cf. ESV). "My eyes fail because of tears" means he cried all the time. "My spirit is greatly troubled" means he grieved not only outwardly in tears, but inside as well. These phrases describe emotional exhaustion. Jeremiah was emotionally wiped out, expressing his own sickness and sorrow because of the horrific consequences of sin (see also Jeremiah 8:18; 9:1; 13:17; 14:17; Lamentations 3:48–49).

As Kaiser aptly writes:

> No one had laboured longer and harder to reverse the destruction-bound forces within the Judean society than God's messenger, Jeremiah. But now that the worst had happened he did not abandon his calloused audience with a weary wave of the hand and a flippant rebuff: "Well, I told you it would happen." God's love and personal regard for this people can be seen in His sending Jeremiah to express his grief at the hurt that came upon his fellow-citizens, nation, and Temple.
>
> "Weep with those who weep"; and weep he did. He mourned until he was worn out and exhausted from weeping. The pain he genuinely felt had enraged his bowels and liver (the organ which in that culture was felt to be the center of intense emotion; in this context, pain).[5]

Because of the destruction of the daughter of my people, when little ones and infants faint / in the streets of the city

The reason for Jeremiah's broken heart is stated and an illustration given. The "destruction [brokenness] of the daughter of my people" is why his eyes failed with tears, his stomach churned, and his inner man was in utter turmoil.

---

5 Kaiser, 70.

The destruction was horrifically illustrated by the "little ones"—children and even "infants" (nursing infants)—who were "faint in the streets of the city." Since Nebuchadnezzar had cut off the supply lines, there was no food except what was already in the city and mothers were forced to produce nourishment for their infants without having ample nourishment for themselves. Evidently even nursing babies found no comfort or nourishment at their mothers' breasts.[6] The helpless of society had to bear the temporal consequences of their parents' sin. Jerusalem was in a horrible, horrible state. Thus Jeremiah expressed his compassionate sorrow and wept profoundly with the weeping city.

VERSE 12

They say to their mothers, "Where is grain and wine?"
As they faint like a wounded man / in the streets of the city

To further portray the scene, Jeremiah goes on to record a poetic conversation between children and their mothers. "Grain and wine" would be the staples of that society (Deuteronomy 11:14). These children were starving to death, losing consciousness "like a wounded man in the streets of the city."

As their life is poured out / on their mothers' bosom

As their helpless mothers held their precious babies, "their life [was] poured out on their mothers' bosom." The NET Bible reads: "They die slowly in their mothers' arms." Think of the grief in these mothers' hearts—they had no means to fulfill the nurturing instinct God had placed within them. What suffering! This is a painful example of the extent of the cruelty of suffering sin brings. As Harrison writes: "This pathetic and tragic scene stands in stark contrast to the ideal of happy, carefree children playing in the streets of Jerusalem, a situation which is promised when the nation is restored (Zechariah 8:5)."[7] As Guest writes: "To see a child suffer was more than he could take. Now he understood, perhaps even thanked God for forbidding him to marry and to procreate."[8]

---

6 Kaiser, 70.

7 R. K. Harrison, *Jeremiah & Lamentations* (Downers Grove, IL: IVP, 1973), 218.

8 Guest, John, *Mastering the Old Testament: Jeremiah, Lamentations,* vol. 17 (Nashville: Word, 1988), 366–67.

Rather than smugly offering an "I told you so," Jeremiah first offered *compassion concerning the pain.*

VERSE 13

How shall I admonish you? To what shall I compare you,
O daughter of Jerusalem? To what shall I liken you as I comfort you,
O virgin daughter of Zion?

Jeremiah here acknowledges the inadequacy of words to fully address Israel's pain and suffering, implying that testimony and comfort can only ultimately come from One greater than him. Comparisons of grief and words of comfort on a human level fall short. The prophet himself is so overcome with grief that he has nothing left to offer to them.

For your ruin is as vast as the sea; who can heal you?

The implied answer has to be, "No one but God Himself." No man can heal a heart and soul that has experienced such loss. But God is able to heal a heart that has experienced this kind of grief. Psalm 147:3 says of God, "He heals the brokenhearted and binds up their wounds."

In speaking these words, Jeremiah reveals compassion, clarity, and realism concerning sin's consequences. From a human perspective, Israel has been damaged beyond measure. The prophet proceeds in verses 14–17 to realistically catalog some of the causes and the consequences and damage.

VERSE 14

Your prophets have seen for you / false and foolish visions

The terms *false* and *foolish* are literally "emptiness" and "whitewash."[9] After clearly and genuinely showing compassion and acknowledging that words cannot fully describe Israel's suffering, the prophet goes on to clarify some of the issues that led to her devastation. Judah's "prophets" taught "emptiness and whitewash." They spoke vain messages that made things look better than they really were;

---

9 Kaiser, 71.

they spoke an "uplifting" message void of sin and judgment (see Jeremiah 5:31; 6:13–14; 14:13–17; 23:11, 16–17, 30–40; 27:14–15).

And they have not exposed your iniquity / so as to restore you from captivity

Jeremiah points out here that Israel's prophets—those who called themselves the spokesmen of God—had not "exposed" their "guilt so as to turn them from captivity" (author's translation). Their message was one of peace and blessing. It was a positive message that did not expose sin or guilt. Consequently, it did not really help those who listened because it was not faithful to God.

In contrast, Jeremiah was faithful to pronounce God's message and paid the price for it. He was beaten and thrown into prison, where he endured the indescribable pain of loneliness that often characterizes the life of a true prophet. He warned the people of God's judgment, but the other prophets did not. Instead, the false prophets contradicted God's promise to give Judah into the hands of the king of Babylon by wrongly promising peace. "For from the least of them even to the greatest of them, everyone is greedy for gain, and from the prophet even to the priest everyone deals falsely. They have healed the brokenness of My people superficially, saying, 'Peace, peace,' but there is no peace" (Jeremiah 6:13–14). But Jeremiah did not preach peace. He cried, "War! War! God is coming to judge you." As a result, God lamented, "They healed the brokenness of My people superficially" (8:11).

But they have seen for you false and misleading oracles

See Jeremiah 28 (cf. 29:8–9; 37:19; Ezekiel 13:1–16; Micah 2:11; 3:5–7). It is false hope to avoid the issue of sin and preach only peace and blessing.

Jeremiah reminds his suffering people that they were deceived by false prophets who did not expose sin, guilt, or error. Rather, these men actually coddled and tacitly promoted the sin that led to Israel's judgment.

VERSE 15

All who pass along the way / clap their hands in derision at you

"All who pass along the way" refer to those non-Israelites who see the city in its now wretched condition. They give it a mocking ovation. If Judah's own grief weren't enough, we now see that her enemies added to the pain by heaping insult upon injury. Ezekiel 25:6–7 says this about Ammon: "Because you have clapped your hands and stamped your feet and rejoiced with all the scorn of your soul against the land of Israel, therefore, behold, I have stretched out My hand against you…" (see also 2 Chronicles 7:21–22).

They hiss and shake their heads / at the daughter of Jerusalem

Hiss can be translated "whistle" as well. Sin had not led to fulfillment but rather degradation, mockery, and disgust (see 1 Kings 9:6–8; Psalm 22:7; 44:14–15; and Jeremiah 19:8).

"Is this the city of which they said, 'The perfection of beauty, a joy to all the earth'?"

Psalm 48:2 says, "Beautiful in elevation, the joy of the whole earth is Mount Zion in the far north, the city of the great King." And Psalm 50:2 says, "Out of Zion, the perfection of beauty, God has shone forth." Jeremiah reminds suffering Jerusalem that because she listened to false prophets and bland prophecies that did not expose sin, the rest of the world now mocks the truth of God. It is too often true that hardened sinners eagerly wait for the demise of the righteous (Psalm 22:7–8).

VERSE 16

All your enemies / have opened their mouths wide against you

The ESV renders this phrase: "All your enemies rail against you" (see Psalm 22:13; 35:21; Lamentations 3:46).

They hiss and gnash their teeth

The enemies also deride and mock with hissing (whistling). Psalm 36:16 says, "Like godless jesters at a feast, they gnashed at me with their teeth." Psalm 37:12 says, "The wicked plots against the righteous and gnashes at him with his teeth." There is both mockery and anger in their whistling, laughing, and vicious words.

They say, "We have swallowed her up! Surely this is the day
for which we waited; we have reached it, we have seen it"
Babylon and the enemy coalition believe they have "swallowed" Judah and Jerusalem. But they fail to recognize that they were only tools in the hand of a
sovereign and holy God (cf. 2:2, 5, 8—"swallowed"; see also Jeremiah 51:34).

VERSE 17

The LORD has done what He purposed; He has accomplished His word /
which He commanded from days of old
This verse is the culmination of the chapter up to this point. Forty times in the
first ten verses, God is referenced in relation to Israel's humiliation.[10] This verse
then succinctly attributes what has happened to the sovereign faithfulness of the
LORD. Jeremiah reminds Jerusalem that Yahweh, the covenant-keeping One,
was simply being faithful to His Word (the covenant curses promised in Leviticus 26:14–46 and Deuteronomy 38:15–68 as well as the commands found in
Leviticus, Deuteronomy, Joshua, and Jeremiah, where specific warnings were
also given as to what would happen if they committed spiritual adultery with
false gods). The point is that it is God who takes responsibility for Israel's calamity. The people of God were indeed responsible for their own sin, but it is God's
purpose that is accomplished in the end.

Zechariah 1:6 may be a reference to what follows in 2:18–19 after this truth
was fully recognized and embraced.

He has thrown down without sparing, and He has caused
the enemy to rejoice over you
The verb "thrown down" or "tear down" was used in verse 2 (cf. also Jeremiah
45:4). See Psalm 89:42 for the enemy rejoicing.

He has exalted the might of your adversaries
The LORD exalted "the horn" of Israel's adversaries while cutting off Israel's
(cf. v. 3).

The believing remnant, listening to Jeremiah's song of sorrow, would

---

10 Kaiser, 63.

remember the covenant faithfulness of Yahweh, the implication being that if Yahweh was faithful in judgment, there is hope of His faithful restoration of all those who call upon Him in faith (cf. Leviticus 26:44–45; Deuteronomy 4:23–31; 30:1–14).

So in verses 18–19, Jeremiah counsels Israel concerning their devastation and the need for faith. In essence, he calls God's people to seek God!

Verse 18

Their heart cried out to the Lord, "O wall of the daughter of Zion"

Some have taken verses 18–19 as Judah's enemies' mocking taunt. It would seem better, considering the larger flow of thought, to see this as Jeremiah's counsel concerning how Israel should respond to God's sovereign discipline.

The phrase "Their heart cried out to *Adonai*" may mean that his audience had finally received the prophet's message and turned in faith to the Sovereign Master. Modern English translations render this first sentence, with some poetic license, as an imperative—"Cry out from your heart to the Lord, O wall of Daughter Zion!" (NET). The Bible in Basic English renders it: "Let your cry go up to the Lord: O wall of the daughter of Zion." The "wall of the daughter of Zion" may be a poetic way of describing all those who had been devastated by the destruction of Judah and Jerusalem. Or it could be in apposition to *Adonai*—a poetic way of telling the daughter of Zion that the Lord is her true wall/protection.

It seems best to understand Jeremiah as calling on Israel to cry out to the Sovereign One in their grief.

"Let your tears run down like a river day and night; give yourself no relief, let your eyes have no rest"

The poet counsels a humiliated and chastened nation to grieve mightily—"day and night," without "relief." The last phrase is literally, "Let not the daughter of thine eye stand still" (YLT). "Don't stop grieving over sin and its consequences before the Lord," seems to be the idea. Jeremiah wasn't advocating endless grief; rather he was warning against letting the grief turn to numbness before fully and completely turning to the Lord, as the next verse indicates. He alone is sovereign; He alone can help.

VERSE 19

"Arise, cry aloud in the night / at the beginning of the night watches"

The "beginning of the night watches" would be sunset–10 p.m.; 10 p.m.–2 a.m.; 2 a.m.–6 a.m.[11] In essence, Jeremiah was calling the people to pray throughout the night. They were to incessantly cry out to God for compassion, for He is "compassionate and gracious, slow to anger and abounding in lovingkindness" (Psalm 103:8). This is the only truly helpful response to grief, pain, suffering, and sorrow.

"Pour out your heart like water / before the presence of the Lord"

In Psalm 62:7–8, the psalmist wrote: "On God my salvation and my glory rest; the rock of my strength, my refuge is in God. Trust in Him at all times, O people; pour out your heart before Him; God is a refuge for us." Jeremiah here exhorts both prayer and faith "before the face of *Adonai*," the Sovereign Master (see the example of Hannah in 1 Samuel 1:15; see also Psalm 142:1–2).

In essence, Jeremiah's counsel is: "Go to the Lord; Go to the Lord; Go to the Lord." The thought is akin to Jacob's persistent prayer in Genesis 32:46: "I will not let You go."

"Lift up your hands to Him / for the life of your little ones / who are faint because of hunger / at the head of every street"

The lifting up of "hands to Him" speaks of prayer, praise, and supplication in the Psalms (28:2; 63:4; 134:2; 141:2). Here the idea of supplication seems to be the strongest. See Isaiah 51:17–20 for the phrase "at the head of every street" in the context of judgment and famine.

The discipleship of the songwriter Jeremiah was one of compassion; clarity and realism concerning sin and its consequences; and counsel to pursue the Lord fully in the midst of grief.

The first movement of chapter 2 recounts the discipline of the Lord. Then the discipleship of the poet is recorded in verses 11–19. In verses 20–22, the third movement in the poem, Jerusalem responds in prayer to the counsel of Jeremiah.

---

11 Theo Laetsch, *Jeremiah* (St. Louis: Concordia, 1952), 386.

VERSE 20

See, O LORD, and look!

The plea "See, O Yahweh" once again surfaces, as in 1:9, 11, 20. This exact phrase, "See, O LORD, and look," was also used in 1:11. It is a call for the merciful gaze of Yahweh to be fixed once more upon His covenant people. First Chronicles 21:15 records the merciful "look" of Yahweh and His relenting care for His own who are experiencing calamity.

At its heart, this is a petition of faith, seeking the mercy of the only One who can truly rescue the destitute, bereft of hope, apart from the mercy of God.

With whom have You dealt thus?

Dealt speaks of dealing with one in severity. As Kaiser notes: "The cry is not one of reproach but a reminder that the incomprehensible aspect of this whole affair is that the Lord had not done this to a pagan nation but to the people and nation of promise."[12] Perhaps the implicit cry is made explicit by the words of Isaiah 64:8–12:

> But now, O LORD, You are our Father, we are the clay, and You our potter; and all of us are the work of Your hand. Do not be angry beyond measure, O LORD, nor remember iniquity forever; behold, look now, all of us are Your people. Your holy cities have become a wilderness, Zion has become a wilderness, Jerusalem a desolation. Our holy and beautiful house, where our fathers praised You, has been burned by fire; and all our precious things have become a ruin. Will You restrain Yourself at these things, O LORD? Will You keep silent and afflict us beyond measure?

Judah is saying, "Look at us. Look at *who* You have done this to. You have done this to *Your* people." What were they doing? They were bringing to their minds the fact that God is a covenant keeper. What sliver of faith that remained reached toward the faithfulness of God. They were admitting, "We don't have anything else to cling to. All is destroyed. Our children have died. We have

---

12 Kaiser, 73.

nothing except God." The next question details the horror of the circumstances but implies faith in Yahweh's compassion.

Should women eat their offspring, the little ones who were born healthy?

See the grotesque prophecies of Leviticus 26:29 and especially Deuteronomy 28:53–57 (cf. also Jeremiah 19:9). In light of these warnings, we must view the suffering the people of God were experiencing as a testimony of God's faithfulness to His own Word. Also, there is an appeal to both the compassion and righteousness of God here, which again implies a measure of faith by the supplicant, as they in essence remind God of the covenant He made with Abraham.

Should priest and prophet be slain / in the sanctuary of the Lord?

Jerusalem was heeding Jeremiah's counsel and pouring out their heart to the Lord—the tragedy, the pain, the horror. No, under normal circumstances "priest and prophet" should not be slain "in the sanctuary of the Lord." But note the words of Ezekiel 9:4–11.

Jerusalem personified asks her questions of the Lord, questions that reveal the horror of her plight yet demonstrate faith in the righteousness and compassion of God.

VERSE 21

On the ground in the streets / lie young and old; my virgins and my young men / have fallen by the sword

Second Chronicles 36:17 says, "Therefore He brought up against them the king of the Chaldeans who slew their young men with the sword in the house of their sanctuary, and had no compassion on young man or virgin, old man or infirm; He gave them all into his hand." The Babylonians waited eighteen months outside the walls of Jerusalem, until the city was starving and the walls could be breached. The waiting no doubt served to intensify their rage.

You have slain them in the day of Your anger, You have slaughtered,
not sparing

But rather than blaming the Chaldeans, the remnant personified acknowledges that it was God's "anger" that brought about this slaughter (see 3:43). God is the One who had done this in the day of His anger. This is a prayer of brutal honesty but not utter faithlessness. Again, if God is sovereign over the misery, then He alone can grant mercy.

VERSE 22

You called as in the day of an appointed feast / my terrors on every side

This is an acknowledgement that God used human agents in His severe punishment. He "called as in the day of an appointed feast." Jerusalem was the feast, and the Chaldeans became Judah's "terrors on every side." There was no escaping the terror. "There had been as much carnage in the city as there was on feast days when the priests slew large quantities of sacrificial animals."[13]

And there was no one who escaped or survived / in the day of
the Lord's anger

The inescapability of God's judgment is graphically pictured in Amos 9:1–4. Certainly there were individual survivors in Jerusalem and elsewhere, but no social or age strata of society escaped judgment. As well, we can be assured in God's sovereignty that "no one" marked for death escaped "in the day of the LORD's anger" (again see Ezekiel 9:4).

Those whom I bore and reared, my enemy annihilated them

The prayer ends with a lament over the death of the children at the hands of the "enemy." Perhaps this is an acknowledgement that because of her sins, Judah had become Yahweh's "enemy." Or else it speaks directly of the Babylonians. Either way, Jerusalem tells the Lord of the loss of her children.

Thus *the song of sovereignty and divine discipline* concludes with tears rather than with a storybook ending of happiness. Yes, the people have recounted the

---

13 *Constable's Expository Notes on the Bible.*

discipline of the Sovereign Lord, heard the discipleship of the songwriter, and poured out their hearts in both faith and devastation, but the pain of loss is still present. Yet these are the steps to dealing with grief and despair.

INSIGHTS FOR COUNSELING

God is love. He would never intentionally bring pain and suffering into my life. Therefore the grief that I experience is from some impersonal force—like fate—something random and out of control. It certainly cannot be from God. He is too good to let me suffer.

So reason many professing Christians.

But the Bible clearly teaches that God is both infinitely good *and* in control of all creation—*even the evil in the world.* Though He is not the author of evil, He is Ruler over it, as the book of Job illustrates. And because God is in control of all things, we can have hope and turn to Him for mercy and grace in the face of overwhelming circumstances.

Jeremiah did not stop with simply recognizing that the Lord was the One who was behind Judah's horrifying circumstances. To simply say, "God did this," and then stop would leave God's people to dangle over the precipice of bitterness and despair. It would inevitably lead to hardness of heart and hopelessness. Instead, as pastor-poet, Jeremiah moved on to shepherd the severely disciplined nation and thus minister a measure of comfort and hope to them.

We, like Jeremiah, have to live with the temporal consequences of sin in a fallen world. But how do we deal with the devastation? We must learn to exercise biblical faith to see our painful circumstances as God's discipline or training rather than as cards dealt out by blind fate (Hebrews 12:5–11).

However, *while* we are in the valley of affliction, we don't always see it this way. When we feel God's heavy hand upon us and day by day face the grievous consequences of our sins, we feel His anger. Deep down we know that He is not pleased. If our chastening is the result of our sin, then we are right to think this way. And it would be wrong for us to dismiss suffering and affliction as an impersonal event that comes upon us without careful thought from God.

When we think about the anger of God, however, we must not equate it with our own expressions of this emotion. Our anger is almost always sinful and is usually sudden or volcanic in nature. But God's anger is different. It is never out of control. Walter Kaiser describes it this way:

> God's anger is never explosive, unreasonable or unexplainable. It is rather His firm expression of real displeasure with our wickedness and sin. Even in God it is never a force or a ruling passion; rather, it is always an instrument of His will. And His anger has not, thereby, shut off his compassion to us (Psalm 77:9). God's anger marks the end of indifference. He cannot and will not remain neutral and impartial in the presence of continued sin.[14]

God's anger "marks the end of indifference." It marks the end of His patience with sinners, and ironically, it also signals the opening of the door to experiencing His mercy. This is the discipleship of Jeremiah—who spoke with compassion yet clarity and realism and counseled his people toward a relentless pursuit of the Lord through their pain. Chapter 2 is rich with biblical principles that move believers to recite the devastation sin has wrought in their lives, even as they seek God and call upon Him with chastened words of faith.

1. When faced with dreadful consequences in life, we tend to dwell on our circumstances and blame the people around us—failing to see our situation as ultimately coming from the hand of God.

If we focus on the human agent of our pain, or on our circumstances, there is no hope for mercy and relief. But if we see our situation in life as from God's hand, we can run to Him with our pain and always have the hope of knowing that He turns His attentive ear to those who tremble at His Word (Isaiah 66:2). It is significant to note that Jeremiah does not even mention the human agents of Jerusalem's destruction. Instead he focuses on the Lord's sovereign chastening and displeasure (Lamentations 2:1–10; Romans 5:3–5; 8:28–29).

---

14 Kaiser, 62.

2. Recognizing God's sovereignty in our circumstances ought to foster genuine humility.

He gives grace to the humble (James 4:6). Sadly, some who recognize God's sovereign discipline harden their hearts to it and get angry with Him and turn away—either in outright rebellion (Jeremiah 44:15–17) or in hopelessness and quiet stubbornness of heart (18:11–12; Ezekiel 37:11). But note David's trust in the sovereign hand of Yahweh, even when wielded in discipline in 1 Chronicles 21:9–13. It is fitting for this trust to produce honest crying out to God for help and hope (Lamentations 2:19).

3. Good counsel will compassionately but realistically point out the truth about sin, guilt, deception, truth, and error.

We must not surround ourselves with counselors or preachers who craft their words to build up our "self-esteem." When we do this, we may feel better superficially, but the deepest needs of our hearts are not addressed (Jeremiah 6:13–14). In order for the heart to be healed, some pain must be inflicted through recognition of the hard truth concerning our sin. (For another example, see Nathan's confrontation of David in 2 Samuel 12:1–7.) The Great Physician and lover of our soul—Jesus—uses His sometimes-painful Word to wound in order that He might heal (Lamentations 2:13–17).

4. We need to be realistic about sin and its consequences and then incessantly cry out to the Lord in our grief.

This is not our natural tendency, but His mercy is our only hope. His faithfulness is our only encouragement. Denying our guilt will get us nowhere except further from God. Like David, we must conclude and pray, "Against You, You only, I have sinned and done what is evil in Your sight" (Psalm 51:1–4). True hope is only found in God as we cry out to Him (Lamentations 2:18–22; Psalm 42:1–11).

5. When we are afflicted for our sins, we oftentimes feel that God is silent because He is silent.

And He is using that silence to bring us to a place of brokenness and repentance so that we will cry out to Him and be restored to fellowship. Affliction gets our attention so that we will hear again the voice of the Lord speaking to us through His Word (Lamentations 2:9; Isaiah 59:1–2).

6. If we are going to learn to respond properly to the discipline God brings into our lives, we must get to the point of realizing that God's anger is righteous.

It is right for God to discipline us. It is right for Him to not let us get away with our sin. We must think correctly about God's right to chasten us when we stray from His Word (Lamentations 2:17; Psalm 119:7, 75, 137; 145:17).

7. We must be careful that our grief does not become self-centered.

When we go through deep suffering, the temptation is to think primarily of ourselves. However, we need to realize that our sin brings suffering on other people as well. Our sin affects everyone around us. Perhaps the most vivid illustration of this principle beyond the book of Lamentations is the story of Achan, whose entire family was stoned for his disobedience (Joshua 7). One person's sin can bring grief into the lives of many (Lamentations 2:11–12).

8. One of the chief purposes of divine discipline is to increase our awareness of the seriousness of sin.

The discipline of God is meant to produce painful regret over sin in order to deter us from repeating our foolish rebellion. Proverbs 13:15 honestly declares, "The way of the unfaithful is hard" (NKJV). Therefore, we must resist the temptation to wish that God would remove the pain *before* His sanctifying work within us is fully accomplished (Lamentations 2:13–17).

9. Sin does not deliver the promises that it claims.

Rather it brings only pain and misery with its rebellion. Its pleasure is but for a moment. Moses knew this; therefore he did not consider the passing pleasures of Egypt to be ultimately worthwhile (Hebrews 11:25). Sin delivers hardship, misery, pain, and ultimately death (Lamentations 2:10; James 1:13–16).

10. If God has brought grievous things into your life, then cry.

There are people who still live in the pain of the past (perhaps over the death of someone dear) because they have never grieved. In the pride of their so-called strength, they have never allowed themselves to be humbled to the point of tears. Jeremiah essentially says, "If God has brought pain into your life, don't be angry and bitter toward Him. Instead cry out to Him. Grieve. Cry rivers of tears before Him." Unfortunately, too many people view tears as a sign of weakness, and that pride will not allow them to be brought to tears of brokenness. However, God wants us to respond to our grief in such a way that we are emptied of self and thereby made ready to be filled with His strength. Like Judah, we must allow our grief to drive us to the compassion of God (Lamentations 1:2; 2:19; Psalm 147:3; 116:5).

11. God uses suffering and affliction to bring us to a place of Godward acceptance.

When we have nothing but God, we have everything we need. If we possess nothing of earthly value but know God through Jesus Christ, we possess everything. We must let our hope rest in the faithfulness and sufficiency of God (Psalm 73:25–26; Philippians 3:7–8). The mercy of God is what we must look to when He is chastening us for our unfaithfulness to Him. We must cry out to Him for mercy. We must tell Him that we know we don't deserve to be treated any better. We must thank Him for the mercy that belongs to us when we belong to Christ (Lamentations 2:17–19; Ephesians 2:4–6).

HOMEWORK FOR COUNSELING

You are encouraged to photocopy homework pages for use in personal counseling.

PART 1: THINKING RIGHTLY ABOUT SIN AND ABOUT GOD

1. As Jeremiah cataloged the causes and consequences of their tribulation (2:14-17), list the specific ways that God has humbled you in your current situation.
2. In what ways have you been tempted to blame others instead of seeing your present circumstances as being from the hand of a sovereign God?
3. Lamentations exhorts the sufferer to persistently cry out to God for mercy. What other avenues of comfort and relief do you find yourself turning to other than God (for example, Internet research, television, alcohol, food, medication, self-pity, etc.)?
4. Psalm 102 is a wonderful example of crying out to God in times of

affliction. Read the psalm, and list (a) the circumstances the psalmist is facing, (b) the emotions he expresses, (c) his right and wrong thoughts concerning God, (d) specific requests made to God, and (e) lessons the psalmist learned or conclusions he reached as a result of his suffering.

5.   Write out your own prayer acknowledging God's sovereignty over your current situation, confessing any known sin and asking Him to intervene with mercy—on His terms, as He decides, rather than according to your own expectations.

PART 2: HOPING IN JESUS

Where do the truths found in Lamentations 2 bring us? To the same place chapter 1 led—hope in Jesus. Why? Apart from Jesus there is no escape from the anger of God. We are sinners. We have gone our own way, against God's authority and in rebellion against His Word. We were once "children of wrath" (Ephesians 2:3). Before conversion we were objects of the wrath of God, but in Christ we have become His children by faith. Why? "God displayed [Jesus] publicly as a propitiation in His blood through faith" (Romans 3:24). This means that Jesus' death fully satisfied the righteous anger of God. This is good news! Jesus Christ, the Son of God, went to the cross to absorb the anger of God so that you and I would not have to. If you are not hoping in Jesus, then there is no hope for you. There is no escape from God's anger if you are not trusting in Jesus, the only One who can protect you from the righteous wrath of God. Jesus willingly became the object of God's wrath so that we would no longer have to be. Paul says in Romans 5:9, "Much more then, having now been justified by His blood, we shall be saved from the wrath of God through Him."

You and I are sinners and therefore deserve the wrath of God to be unleashed upon us in unlimited ways. However, in His mercy, He chose to pour out His righteous anger on His blameless Son instead of on us. As Jesus hung on the cross, our sins were laid upon Him and He was put to death in our place. Is this the Jesus you are hoping in? Is this the Jesus you are resting in? If it isn't, then you've got the wrong Jesus. On the other hand, if you are trusting in the Lord Jesus Christ as the One who bore the penalty of your sin before a holy God, then you have already been released from the anger of God.

- Read 2 Corinthians 5:17–21.

1. What is continuously taking place in the person who is a new creature in Christ?

2. What does it mean that God has reconciled believers to Himself through Christ?

3. Explain the wondrous exchange mentioned in verse 21.

4. Write your own paraphrase of verse 21 in the first person (I, me, my).

As believers in Christ, it is significant to realize that although the eternal judgment for our sins has already been fully taken from us by the sacrifice of Jesus, the temporal consequences of our sin often remain. As His children, God lovingly disciplines us when we sin by allowing us to suffer the consequences of our sin. He does this in order to train us to live in righteousness for His glory (Hebrews 12:10–11; 2 Timothy 3:16–17).

"I AM THE MAN WHO HAS SEEN AFFLICTION"

A Song of Suffering, Dependence, and Determined Hope

Lamentations 3:1–18

C hapter 3 is the heart and soul of the book of Lamentations. Its structure is different than the other four chapters in that it has sixty-six verses, while the others have twenty-two verses mainly arranged as an acrostic built upon the letters of the Hebrew alphabet. But in the third chapter, three verses are given to each letter, giving us sixty-six verses in all. This first section of chapter 3 enumerates the suffering of the poet-servant. It is a brutal assessment of life under the chastening hand of God. From the human perspective, there was only pain, sorrow, and despair. Jeremiah captures the sense of being barely alive in the prison of regret, fearing that all hope is gone.

But with the final words of 3:17–18, it would seem that despite the suffering servant's human assessment of hopelessness, "hope from Yahweh" caused him to humbly pray (vv. 19–20) and then remember the truth about Yahweh and His loyal love, His faithful mercies. As Kaiser writes: "This robust outburst of despair, however, is followed immediately by the first sighs that form the basis of his prayer and his hope for the future."[1]

Too often, Christianity is portrayed as a magic pill that will somehow make your life problem-free—if you just have enough faith. But the book of Lamentations, particularly chapter 3, reveals that even believers can be overwhelmed by grievous circumstances and overcome by feelings of despair. And when we are, our only recourse is to detail our pain and sorrow—and God's sovereignty over it—and embrace by faith the unceasing love and absolute sufficiency of the Lord. In seeing before us the open maw of hopelessness and ruin, believers are left with only one way of escape: remembering in faith what we know to be true from God's Word and humbling ourselves in the grip of His sovereign but gracious hand.

In Lamentations 3:1–18, we see six movements that summarize the sufferer's assessment of God's extreme discipline from the human point of view. It is a perspective that is quite blunt concerning pain, sorrow, and despair.

TEACHING OUTLINES

Option A

   I. A song of sorrow and despair (1:1–22)

  II. A song of sovereignty and divine discipline (2:1–22)

III. A song of suffering and determined dependence (3:1–66)

     A. The suffering of the servant enumerated [The man of sorrows] (3:1–18)

        1. The hand of God (vv. 1–3)

          a. The divine discipline of the rod of His wrath (v. 1)

          b. The divine discipline of darkness (v. 2)

          c. The divine discipline of the hand of God (v. 3)

        2. The hardships (vv. 4–7)

          a. Broken health (v. 4)

          b. Bitterness and hardship (v. 5)

          c. Burial (v. 6)

          d. Bondage (v. 7)

        3. The helplessness (vv. 8–9)

---

1 Walter C. Kaiser, Jr., *Grief and Pain in the Plan of God* (Fearn: Christian Focus, 2004), 88.

   a. My prayers are shut out (v. 8)
   b. My paths are blocked and crooked (v. 9)
4. The horror (vv. 10–13)
   a. Torn to pieces (vv. 10–11)
   b. Targeted and pierced (vv. 12–13)
5. The humiliation (vv. 14–16)
   a. The songs of mocking (v. 14)
   b. The satiation of bitterness (v. 15)
   c. The stature of defeat (v. 16)
6. The hopelessness (vv. 17–18)
   a. The absence of peace and happiness (v. 17)
   b. The assessment based upon circumstances and feelings (v. 18)

Option B

I. We must respond to affliction with honesty and humility (vv. 1–20)
   A. Honesty about God's discipline (vv. 1–18)
      1. His hand of blessing has turned into a fist of wrath (vv. 1–3)
      2. His healing touch has brought hardship (vv. 4–6)
      3. His hearing ear has become a silent prison (vv. 7–9)
      4. His fellowship has turned into hostility (vv. 10–12)
      5. His acceptance has been replaced by rejection (vv. 13–15)
      6. His peace has turned into fear and despair (vv. 16–18)

EXPOSITION
VERSE 1

I am the man who has seen affliction / because of the rod of His wrath

Chapter 3 is the centerpiece of the entire book of Lamentations. It is unique in both content and form. Whereas the other chapters have twenty-two verses, chapter 3 has sixty-six. The acrostics of chapters 1, 2, and 4 follow the alphabet normally, except the previously mentioned *peh* and *ayin* reversal (see introduction). Chapter 3, however, is arranged in triplets—the first three verses begin with *aleph,* the next three *beth,* etc.

The declaration "I am the man" appropriately introduces chapter 3 as unique in content as well. Jeremiah writes in the first person, evidently revealing his personal pain and suffering yet somehow maintaining corporate solidarity with the suffering nation (see 3:22, 40–47 [plural pronouns], then back to first person in 3:48–63[2]). He is not identifying personal guilt as the cause of the destruction. He is the faithful prophet. Judah, not Jeremiah, is guilty—of stiffening her neck and hardening her heart against the Lord. However, as a faithful prophet, Jeremiah takes upon himself the sin burden of the people he serves. As part of Judah, he too suffers. The prophet "spoke as if the judgment from God fell directly on Jeremiah himself. He uses the first person pronouns 'I' and 'me' and the possessive pronouns 'my' and 'mine' seventy-two times in this chapter."[3]

Notably, the standard Hebrew term for *man* is not used here, but rather a word that communicates man in his strength—"I am the mighty man." The same term is used in Psalms 34:8 and 40:4 to refer to the man who trusts in the Lord. In Psalm 52:7, it is used of the "mighty man" who would *not* trust in the Lord. And in Psalm 94:12 it refers to the man who is blessed by the chastening or discipline of the Lord. Perhaps Psalm 88:4 employs the word in parallel fashion and similar context:

> For my soul has had enough troubles, and my life has drawn near to Sheol. I am reckoned among those who go down to the pit; I have become like a man [*geber*/mighty man] without strength, forsaken among the dead, like the slain who lie in the grave, whom You remember no more, and they are cut off from Your hand. You have put me in the lowest pit, in dark places, in the depths. Your wrath has rested upon me, and You have afflicted me with all Your waves. (Psalm 88:3–7)

In light of the immediately following context, it may well be that Jeremiah wanted to subtly highlight the fact that man in his strength is still subject to God's chastening rod.

Perhaps Lamentations gives us some insight into the sufferings of our Lord Jesus as well. He was truly the mighty man of faith who saw "affliction" individually and yet wholly identified with His people. His affliction was beyond that of

---

2 Kaiser, 78.
3 John Hartog, *The Fall of a Kingdom* (Schaumburg: Regular Baptist Press, 1983), 121.

any other man. It is also interesting to note the affliction of the "rod" mentioned in Psalm 89:32 concerning David's sons' disobedience (cf. 2 Samuel 7:14). The word *rod* refers to the chastening of God and is also used in this way by Job. Even though Job's affliction was not the result of his own sin, he cried out in desperation, "Let Him remove His rod from me, and let not dread of Him terrify me" (Job 9:34). The imagery of God's "rod" is also found in Isaiah 10:5.

Notably, the pronoun *He* is used in reference to God throughout the section, except for verse 18. But in the latter portion of chapter 3, the divine names Yahweh and Adonai are frequently used.[4] The result is that the first section is distanced from the covenant Name, and thus hope is quite distant as well. But when Yahweh's covenant-keeping mercies are remembered in verse 22, hope is restored.

As well, the first person pronouns *I, me,* or *my* are used over thirty times in the first eighteen verses. Here is Jeremiah's reflection on the destruction. Thus, this is the most personal portion of the book. Here we see the human perspective of suffering from the sufferer himself. Not surprisingly, then, with the distant pronoun for God, and the intense self-focus, verse 18 ends with a claim of hopelessness.

Jeremiah begins by affirming that indeed he has seen "affliction"—even poverty and humiliation—because of divine chastening.

VERSE 2

He has driven me and made me walk / in darkness and not in light
The word *driven* is elsewhere used of herding and leading flock animals (Genesis 31:18; Exodus 3:1). "But here," notes Mackay, "the Lord is no longer the shepherd who provides abundant green pastures for his people and who leads them beside still waters (Psalm 23:2). Rather his wrath had brought about a reversal of their circumstances, and as a member of the community the poet had shared their destiny."[5] Jeremiah had once proclaimed: "Give glory to the LORD your God, before He brings darkness; and before your feet stumble on the dusky mountains, and while you are hoping for light He makes it into deep darkness,

4   A. W. Streane, "Jeremiah and Lamentations" in *Cambridge Bible for Schools and Colleges* (London: Cambridge University Press, 1952), 347.

5   John L. Mackay. *Lamentations: A Mentor Commentary* (Fearn: Christian Focus, 2008), 127.

and turns it into gloom" (Jeremiah 13:16). Now he too must suffer for the sins of his people (see also Amos 5:18–20; cf. Job 30:25–26).

VERSE 3

Surely against me He has turned His hand / repeatedly all the day

The wording is emphatic. Jeremiah, as God's representative of the people, was experiencing divine discipline from the hand of God "repeatedly all the day." Isaiah 1:25 promised: "I will also turn My hand against you, and will smelt away your dross as with lye and will remove all your alloy." The hand that had delivered Israel in the past was now turned in repeated discipline. The hand that had touched Jeremiah's mouth so as to fill it with the Word of God (Jeremiah 1:9), was now striking the prophet with painful chastening.

VERSE 4

He has caused my flesh and my skin to waste away, He has broken my bones

The wasting away of "flesh" and "skin" and "broken...bones" may speak of loss of weight and literal breaches of health (Job 16:8; 19:20). Yet, while there is no question of Israel's physical suffering, this appears to be figurative speech used to speak metaphorically of intense pain and emotional anguish—like that used by David when he confessed his immorality to God and pleaded, "Make me to hear joy and gladness, let the bones which You have broken rejoice" (Psalm 51:8). David also longed for his crushed spirit to rejoice again (cf. Psalm 32). See also Job 30:17, 30; Psalm 31:9–10; 32:3; 38:2–8; 42:10; 51:8; 102:3–5; Isaiah 38:13; Jeremiah 50:17.

VERSE 5

He has besieged and encompassed me with bitterness and hardship

Literally, this verse reads: "He has built up and surrounded me with poison and hardship." The word *hardship* can refer to weariness and travail. Jeremiah experienced divine judgment like that of a city surrounded by an army that builds siege ramps. He felt poisoned and weary from the pain. Deuteronomy 29:18

predicted that God would bring the poison of bitterness into the lives of His people if they rebelled against Him (also see Jeremiah 8:14).

Verse 6

In dark places He has made me dwell, like those who have long been dead

This verse is nearly an exact quote of Psalm 143:3c: "He has made me dwell in dark places like those who have long been dead." This psalm captures Jeremiah's sense of complete disclosure and honesty about God's discipline and the bitter taste of suffering. See also Psalm 88:3–6, where the "lowest pit" (hell) is associated with the "dark places."

"So deep was his agony of soul and body that he felt as hopeless as those who had died long ago and are now in the grip not only of the grave, but even more tragically in the grip of hell."[6] As John Brown of Haddington wrote, "Saints can never enter the lowest hell, being preserved by grace: but, by multiplied troubles from God, from devils, and from men, they may have a hell upon earth."[7]

Verse 7

He has walled me in so that I cannot go out; He has made my chain heavy

It would seem that Jeremiah was familiar once again with Job's suffering as he penned this verse. Job 19:8 says, "He has walled up my way so that I cannot pass, and He has put darkness on my paths" (cf. also Job 3:23). The references to being "walled...in" and a "chain" refer to either literal or metaphorical bondage. Jeremiah and the nation both experienced captivity and bondage.

More than once he had been thrown into solitary confinement for preaching the Word of God. Jeremiah 38:6 records one experience of incarceration Jeremiah experienced: "Then they took Jeremiah and cast him into the cistern of Malchijah the king's son, which was in the court of the guardhouse; and they let Jeremiah down with ropes. Now in the cistern there was no water but only mud, and Jeremiah sank into the mud." Jeremiah 37:15–16 describes another: "Then the officials were angry at Jeremiah and beat him, and they put him in

---

6 Kaiser, 86.
7 John Brown, *The Self-Interpreting Bible*, 1890 edition, 711.

jail in the house of Jonathan the scribe, which they had made into the prison. For Jeremiah had come into the dungeon, that is, the vaulted cell; and Jeremiah stayed there many days." Evidently he was in fear for his life during that prison stay (see also Jeremiah 37:17–21).

Here the prophet referenced the *hardships* of broken health, bitterness, burial, and bondage. The hardships left him feeling helpless.

Verse 8

Even when I cry out and call for help, He shuts out my prayer

Just as Jeremiah felt abandoned when thrown into prison by his enemies, so the man who is afflicted feels as though he is in a silent prison where nobody hears his cry—not even God. Again Jeremiah may have been alluding to Jeremiah 19: "Behold, I cry, 'Violence!' but I get no answer, I shout for help, but there is not justice" (v. 7). Or perhaps to Job 30:20: "I cry out to You for help, but You do not answer me; I stand up, and You turn Your attention against me."

In the midst of such dire and painful circumstances, the prophet and no doubt the nation thought that even prayer was of no avail.

Verse 9

He has blocked my ways with hewn stone; He has made my paths crooked

"Hewn stone" implies a purposed, immovable obstruction, rather than a temporary or accidental delay.[8] An utter sense of frustration and confusion had overtaken the prophet and his people. The wording is somewhat similar to verse 7, except here the picture is of a traveler facing a divine roadblock with no way of escape. He is lost, confused, frustrated, and open to attack in his wanderings.[9] Jeremiah's life was like being lost in a maze with no way out.[10]

---

8 Mackay, 130.
9 Kaiser, 87.
10 H. L. Ellison, "Lamentations" in *The Expositor's Bible Commentary*, ed by Frank E. Gaebelein (Grand Rapids: Zondervan), 718.

VERSE 10

He is to me like a bear lying in wait, like a lion in secret places

Jeremiah often employed the imagery of a lion to depict Israel's enemies during the course of His ministry (Jeremiah 4:7; 5:6; 49:19; 50:44; cf. Psalm 10:9; 17:12). But here the lion has turned on Judah herself, as the sweetness of God's fellowship has now turned into sour enmity. This is what Jeremiah had prophesied earlier:

> I will go to the great and will speak to them, for they know the way of the LORD and the ordinance of their God. But they too, with one accord, have broken the yoke and burst the bonds. Therefore a lion from the forest will slay them, a wolf of the deserts will destroy them, a leopard is watching their cities. Everyone who goes out of them will be torn in pieces, because their transgressions are many, their apostasies are numerous. (Jeremiah 5:5–6)

He describes the judgment of God upon Judah and Jerusalem as being like that of wild animals that tear him to pieces: "[God] has made me desolate." John Calvin writes, "There is nothing more dreadful than to feel that God is angry with us."[11] Other Scriptures allude to this as well—see for example Job 10:16; Isaiah 38:13; Hosea 5:14; 13:7–8; and especially Amos 5:18–20.

VERSE 11

He has turned aside my ways and torn me to pieces; He has made me desolate

This verse finishes the thought of verse 10. Jeremiah felt like God's discipline was akin to the attack of a wild animal that had dragged him off the path and mangled him, leaving him without help (cf. NIV).

---

11 John Calvin, *Calvin's Commentaries: Volume XI* (Grand Rapids: Baker Books, 2005), 391.

VERSE 12

He bent His bow / and set me as a target for the arrow

Here the metaphor changes from being hunted and mauled by a wild animal to being hunted and shot by an archer. God, designated by the distant pronoun *He,* had "bent His bow and set [Jeremiah and the nation collectively] as a target for the arrow," it would seem. Again, Jeremiah seems to echo the sentiments of Job (see Job 7:20; 16:12–13). See also Psalm 7:12–13.

VERSE 13

He made the arrows of His quiver / to enter into my inward parts

Not only does the sufferer feel like a target for the Almighty's chastening, the divine "arrows of His quiver" actually "enter into [his] inward parts." God had made Jerusalem His target because of her sin. Jeremiah speaks of the inner pain that accompanies God's discipline. It is not merely the outward destruction of the city, but inward pain as well (see Deuteronomy 32:23; Job 6:4; Psalm 38:2).

VERSE 14

I have become a laughingstock to all my people, their song all the day

This verse seems to make the most dramatic distinction in the chapter between the prophet and the people he is identifying with.[12] They sang songs of mocking "all the day" concerning him. The same word for "laughingstock" is used in Job 12:4, there translated "joke": "I am a joke to my friends, the one who called on God and He answered him; the just and blameless man is a joke" (cf. also Job 30:1–9; Psalm 2:6–8; 35:16; 69:12). Perhaps after the destruction of Jerusalem, Jeremiah experienced the same type of mocking. The prophet of God who had warned them was now suffering through the same things with them—how magnanimous of Jeremiah's supposedly sovereign God. Jesus knew this scorn as well (Matthew 27:39–44). Jeremiah 20:7–10 reveals that Jeremiah was the object of scorn before the captivity. Sadly, Israel was a joke to all the "people" whose gods she had embraced in idolatrous lust (Jeremiah 48:27).

---

12 See Mackay's discussion of a possible textual emendation, Mackay, 132.

VERSE 15

*He has filled me with bitterness, He has made me drunk
with wormwood*

Earlier in Jeremiah's ministry, he had proclaimed the Word of God concerning
the false prophets and their future of bitterness and wormwood. Jeremiah 23:15
says, "Therefore thus says the LORD of hosts concerning the prophets, 'Behold,
I am going to feed them wormwood and make them drink poisonous water, for
from the prophets of Jerusalem pollution has gone forth into all the land.'" He
had pronounced the same for Israel: "Therefore thus says the LORD of hosts, the
God of Israel, 'Behold, I will feed them, this people, with wormwood and give
them poisoned water to drink'" (9:15). Now Jeremiah felt that he was satiated
with "bitterness" and "wormwood."

Job 9:18 records these words of suffering: "He will not allow me to get my
breath, but saturates me with bitterness." For Job and Jeremiah, in their suffering was constant bitterness of soul. Wormwood was evidently a plant or shrub
that gave an intensely bitter flavoring. It was considered poisonous in some
contexts. Here the prophet describes himself as "drunk with wormwood."

VERSE 16

He has broken my teeth with gravel; He has made me cower in the dust

The NLT renders this first phrase, "He has made me chew on gravel," which
seems to capture the sense of the Hebrew. Some suggest that the bread of the
impoverished was mixed with tiny pieces of gravel or sand. Proverbs 20:17 says,
"Bread obtained by falsehood is sweet to a man, but afterward his mouth will be
filled with gravel." Sin is sweet when first tasted, but the suffering that results is
compared with chewing stones. And Kaiser notes, "The people had been feeding
on the stones of Baal worship instead of the bread of the Word of God."[13] Instead
of bread, they got stones to eat. The language may, however, reflect the defeated
person lying facedown in the dirt.

Whatever the exact imagery, this is no doubt language of defeat and poverty.
The word *dust* is literally "ashes." Jeremiah was experiencing defeat, poverty, and

---

13 Kaiser, 87.

mourning as he identified with God's people. How much more would Jesus suffer? The thought is overwhelming.

Jeremiah sang of the hand of God against him, the hardships, the helplessness, the humiliation. And these led him to a feeling of hopelessness, as verses 17–18 reveal.

VERSE 17

My soul has been rejected from peace; I have forgotten happiness

Verse 17 serves as a summary and verse 18 a pronouncement concerning the prophet's self-assessed condition. His soul had been "rejected" or deprived of *shalom*. To the Hebrews, peace was not just the absence of conflict, but a wholeness or completeness of life that included blessing—both physical and spiritual. Jeremiah, in his pain and suffering, felt like his very life had "been rejected from" such "peace."

The word *happiness* is literally "good." All good and "prosperity" (KJV) was now removed and "forgotten." The poetic figure is not one of amnesia or a total absence of memories,[14] but of pain so overwhelming that he had forgotten what happiness was.

VERSE 18

So I say, "My strength has perished, and so has my hope from the LORD"

The word translated "so I say" reveals Jeremiah's human assessment of his situation based upon circumstances. He had come to the end of himself. His "strength," or glory, had been destroyed. And so had his "hope from Yahweh." The NET Bible has an interesting rendering of this verse: "So I said, 'My endurance has expired; I have lost all hope of deliverance from the LORD.'" But in finally referring to Yahweh by name rather than pronoun, Jeremiah ignites a spark that will illumine the utter darkness and turn attention to the One who is Hope. In declaring his hopelessness, the poet faces the discipline of God with pure forthrightness.

---

14 Mackay, 134–5.

Insights for Counseling

Hope is a wonderful virtue…when you have it.

Hope is energizing…when you have something in which to place your confidence.

But what about the times when hope has disappeared? When you feel God's heavy hand of discipline upon your life to such an intense degree that all hope flees from your mind and heart? When the dark cloud of despair hangs over you so that you can no longer see the sun? What about the times when you have lost the will to go on? It's times like these, when all appears hopeless, that the Word of God must be our rock-solid foundation, specifically the confirmation and recitation of the truth of God's character and salvation. Hope is found in the Person of God and in the conscious decision to look away from self and to God.

Lamentations 3:1–18 teaches us that while we can certainly describe the pain and horror of our circumstances, we must not become enamored with morbid sorrow, bitterness, and grief. We must not begin to love bitterness of soul, which turns to worship of self. Jeremiah did not stop with sorrow. Instead he remembered the truth—Yahweh is Hope. He prayed in his humiliation (vv. 19–20). And he remembered and recited the truth of God as revealed in His Word. He contemplated Yahweh's character and confirmed His sufficiency, recognizing satisfaction comes only from Him, no matter the temporal circumstances.

In considering what Jeremiah wrote here under the inspiration of the Holy Spirit, we must not ignore the plain parallel between Jeremiah and the Lord Jesus Christ. Jeremiah is the "man who has seen affliction" (v. 1), the man of sorrows, and we are reminded of Isaiah 52:13–53:12 (and specifically Isaiah 53:6)—*the* Man of Sorrows—the One who bore the infinite and eternal rod of God's wrath on behalf of sinners. To this point, Warren Wiersbe has written:

> The ministries of both Jeremiah and Jesus were rejected by the people and both men wept over the city of Jerusalem because they knew that destruction was coming. Both were hated without cause (Lam. 3:52; John 15:25; Ps. 69:4) and both were ridiculed by the leaders (Lam. 3:14; Ps. 69:12). Jeremiah was rejected by his family (Jer. 11:18–23) and Jesus by His family (John 7:1–8). Both Jeremiah and Jesus emphasized a "heart religion" and not just ritual, and both taught by means

of visual images and used common objects and activities to instruct the people. The Jewish leaders rejected the messages of both Jeremiah and Jesus, and the prophet ended up in Egypt and Jesus on a Roman cross. In their day, both were considered miserable failures, but history has proved that both were right.[15]

Jeremiah certainly suffered during and after the fall of Jerusalem to Babylon. But in an infinitely greater way, Jesus identified with His people as He suffered for their sins. And praise God that He did. For in doing so, He took the eternal punishment due us—and we receive the healing of forgiveness, full and free (Isaiah 52:14; 53:3–6, 8–12). On the cross, Jesus cried, "My God, My God, why have You forsaken Me?" (Mark 15:24). Jesus experienced infinite and eternal hopelessness, and His infinite and eternal righteousness swallowed it up so that we could experience everlasting hope in fellowship with God.

Just before He gave up His spirit, Jesus expressed the reality of renewed fellowship with His Father when He said, "Father, into Your hands I commit My spirit" (Luke 23:46). Never stop at temporal hopelessness. Remember the Lord. In remembering you will see new mercies.

1. All suffering is ultimately governed by God, whose sovereign plan is for His glory and our good.

Notice how many times in 3:1–17 Jeremiah acknowledges God as the ultimate source of his pain and his city's destruction. We will *never* begin to reap spiritual profit from our pain if we do not give God glory for who He is and by faith choose to submit to His infinite wisdom. Submitting to God in our suffering means being able to say from our hearts, "And we know that God causes all things to work together for good to those who love God, to those who are called according to His purpose" (Lamentations 3:1–17; Romans 8:28).

---

15 Warren W. Wiersbe, "Lamentations" in *The Bible Exposition Commentary* (Colorado Springs: Cook Communications, 2002), 153.

2. Responding to affliction in a God-pleasing way requires honesty and humility.

When God brings us to the point where all hope is gone, when we look at our lives and our circumstances and exclaim, "This is hopeless, Lord. There is nothing good in what is going on," then we are ready to face His discipline with sincerity, to stop playing charades, and to get honest with God. We must come to the point of saying, "Lord, this is how You are treating me, but it is how I deserve to be treated." We cannot know the hope of the Lord until we are brought to brokenness and true repentance (Lamentations 3:1–18; 2 Corinthians 7:10).

3. When we refuse to turn from our sin, because we love and cherish it, God shuts His ear to our prayers.

For example, Isaiah 59:1–2 says, "Behold, the LORD's hand is not so short that it cannot save; nor is His ear so dull that it cannot hear. But your iniquities have made a separation between you and your God, and your sins have hidden His face from you so that He does not hear." Notice that it does not say that God *cannot* hear; it says that He *does not* hear. God willfully chooses not to listen. Psalm 66:18 agrees: "If I regard wickedness in my heart, the Lord will not hear." If we love our sin more than we love God, then He will not listen to our prayers. Why? It is part of His discipline, which is always for the purpose of restoration, to call us back to an obedient walk with Him. God refuses to answer to get our attention and provoke us to return to Him (Lamentations 3:7–9).

4. When we cherish sin in our hearts, fellowship is lost and we become practical enemies of God.

This principle is taught by both Peter and James: "He is opposed to the proud" (1 Peter 5:5; James 4:6). God fights against us when we are proud in order to break our stubborn wills and bring us to repentance. If we have turned from our sin and to Christ, the One who bore our punishment on the Cross, then we are no longer *positional* enemies of God (Colossians 1:21; 2:13–14). We are now His children, and our position before Him will never change (Romans 8:1; 1 John 3:1–2). However, pride can make us enemies of God in our practice (*practical* enemies of God), as God uses whatever means necessary to humble us.

This discipline is motivated by love. God loves us too much to allow us to remain in our stubbornness. Sin deceives us, promising untold pleasure without allowing us to peek into the destruction that awaits us if we give in to its temptation. But God knows the end of sin. Love for us motivates Him to use pain to spare us from the destruction sin brings (Lamentations 3:7-9; Proverbs 3:11–12).

Homework for Counseling

You are encouraged to photocopy homework pages for use in personal counseling.

Part 1: Thinking Rightly About Sin and About God

1. Keep a journal this week of every time you have felt overwhelmed or depressed by your circumstances. Write at least three-quarters of a page describing your thoughts at the time, your feelings, what you were doing when you first noticed those feelings, and how you responded to them. This will help you better discern any patterns of thinking that are not in keeping with the truth of God's Word.

2. In light of Lamentations 3:1–18, how does your thinking about sin and about God need to change? List specific ways this study has renewed your mind to think biblically.

3. Meditate on Psalm 66:18 and 77:13. How and why is *unconfessed* sin an obstacle to effective prayer? Do you have any sins you have been cherishing in your heart rather than confessing? Take them to the Lord in humble prayer and repentance.

4. Psalm 6 is an example of honest confession to the Lord. Read and meditate on this psalm. Pray it back to God, personalizing it, confessing specific sins as needed, and thanking God for His forgiveness that is based in the sacrifice of Christ on the cross.

Part 2: Hoping in Jesus

God is a God of mercy, but this mercy is only found in Jesus Christ. He is the fountainhead of God's mercy (Ephesians 2:4–5).

1. Consider the similarities between the suffering Jesus endured and the

suffering Jeremiah describes.

- Jesus endured the rod of God's wrath—not for His sin, but for ours (Romans 3:25; 2 Corinthians 5:21; 1 John 2:2).
- Jesus endured a life of hardship and pain (Isaiah 53:3; Matthew 8:20).
- Jesus experienced the imprisonment of loneliness (Matthew 26:56).
- Jesus relinquished fellowship with God when He took our sin upon Himself. He was rejected by His Father so we could be accepted by Him (Mark 15:34; 2 Corinthians 5:21).
- Jesus was rejected, hated, and despised by men (1 Peter 2:23).
  Can you think of any other similarities?

2. Read 1 Peter 2:24; 3:18. What is the purpose of Jesus' sufferings?
3. Read Hebrews 4:15–16. Think about the ministry of Jesus as every believer's High Priest. In the midst of your pain and misery, you may be tempted to think that no one understands or cares.

- How do these verses correct your thinking?
- What comfort do these truths provide?
- What is one way to respond in your times of testing?
- How does remembering Jesus give you strength in the midst of suffering?

Chapter 4

"GREAT IS THY FAITHFULNESS"

The Steadfast Love of the Lord Embraced

Lamentations 3:19–39

Jeremiah enumerated his suffering in detail in Lamentations 3:1–18—to the point of despair (v. 18). After praying in humility and remembering the truth of God's Word, he found himself agreeing with God about His mercy, grace, faithfulness, worthiness, trustworthiness, goodness, justice, sovereignty, and man's sin. In this, Jeremiah found hope.

If we seek the hope Jeremiah found, we must heed his exhortation to turn our eyes *from* the inward gaze that suffering seems to inevitably lead to and *toward* the wondrous truth and grace of God. This only happens when we cry out for mercy and humble our souls before Him. And it will only happen to the degree that His Word directs our thoughts. We must view our circumstances, no matter how desperate they may seem, through the lens of Scripture. We must get our eyes off ourselves—in whom there is no deliverance—and onto the God of the Bible, the only Deliverer.

This isn't an easy three-step program for psychological "healing," success, and happiness. It involves embracing pain by faith, believing that God's ways are perfect. It involves embracing humiliation and reproach. It is something that must be pursued incessantly, by faith, believing that the Lord is good to those who wait for Him, to those who seek Him.

In Lamentations 3:19–39, we will see four movements that reveal the hope found in the Lord in spite of overwhelming and seemingly hopeless circumstances. *This is the centerpiece and crown jewel of the entire book.*

TEACHING OUTLINES

Option A
Seeking God in the Wake of Sin's Misery
  I.   A song of sorrow and despair (1:1–22)
  II. A song of sovereignty and divine discipline (2:1–22)
 III. A song of suffering and determined hope (3:1–66)
     A. The suffering of the servant enumerated [The man of sorrows] (vv. 1–18)
     B. The steadfast love of the LORD embraced [The LORD of hope] (vv. 19–39)
       1. A plea for mercy (v. 19)
       2. A prostration of soul (v. 20)
       3. A proclamation of hope/faith in Yahweh's character no matter the circumstances (v. 21–24)
          a. Remembering the truth (vv. 21–23a)
            i. Turning your heart to the truth (v. 21)
            ii. Taking refuge in the unfailing love and compassion of Yahweh (v. 22–23a)
          b. Renewing worship (v. 23b)
          c. Reaffirming satisfaction in the LORD alone (v. 24)
       4. A prescription for hope/faith in the face of adversity and affliction (vv. 25–39)
          a. Remember that the LORD is good to those who trust and seek Him (vv. 25–27)
            i. The LORD is good to those who wait for Him and seek Him (v. 25)
            ii. The longsuffering of the believer is good (v. 26)

        iii. The load God lays upon the believer is good (v. 27)

    b. Receive the Lord's chastening rather than fight against it (vv. 28–30)

        i. Without complaint (v. 28)

        ii. Willingly accepting humiliation (v. 29)

        iii. Willingly accepting reproach (v. 30)

    c. Remember that the Lord's compassion and abundant lovingkindness will outweigh any affliction (vv. 31–33)

        i. He will not reject forever (v. 31)

        ii. He will have abundant compassion (v. 32)

        iii. He does not take pleasure in causing grief (v. 33)

    d. Remember that the Lord is righteous, and He will not approve of injustice (vv. 34–36)

        i. He does not approve of oppression and bondage (v. 34)

        ii. He does not approve of injustice in heaven (v. 35)

        iii. He does not approve of injustice on earth (v. 36)

    e. Remember that the Lord is ultimately in control of all things (vv. 37–38)

        i. He is sovereign over all things that come to pass (v. 37)

        ii. He is sovereign over both good and ill (v. 38)

    f. Remember what you really deserve in light of your sins (v. 39)

Option B

I. We must respond to affliction with honesty and humility (vv. 1–20)

    A. Honesty about God's discipline (vv. 1–18)

    B. Humility before God's discipline (vv. 19–20)

II. We must remember the mercy and faithfulness of God (vv. 21–24)

III. We must receive chastening from the loving hand of God (vv. 25–39)

    A. Like Jeremiah, we must seek the Lord (vv. 25–27)

    B. Like Jeremiah, we must submit to the Lord's discipline (vv. 28–33)

    C. Like Jeremiah, we must support what the Lord approves (vv. 34–36)

    D. Like Jeremiah, we must surrender to the sovereign Lord (vv. 37–39)

        1. God is sovereign over all things (v. 37)

        2. God is sovereign over good and evil (v. 38)

        3. God is sovereign over sin's judgment (v. 39)

EXPOSITION
VERSE 19

Remember my affliction and my wandering, the wormwood and bitterness

Though the Septuagint version has "I remember my affliction..." (as does the NIV), the Hebrew word is in the imperative—"Remember my affliction." The NASB rightly translates this as a plea. In 3:1–18, the prophet was consumed with his painful circumstances. Though he had almost lost all hope (v. 18), the mention of the covenant name Yahweh at the end of verse 18 led Jeremiah to cry out to God in prayer.

The prophet asks God to "remember"—another way of saying, "Lord, remember me. Do not forget about me. Don't be indifferent to my affliction. Remember me in this time of bitterness." Jeremiah knew intimately his and his people's deep poverty of spirit. The word *wandering* was translated "homelessness" in 1:7. "Wormwood" was used in 3:15 (cf. Jeremiah 9:15; 23:15). "Bitterness" was referenced in 3:5 and translated "poisonous" or "poison" in Deuteronomy 29:18; 32:32–33.

Though nearly hopeless, Jeremiah calls out for mercy one more time. He asks God to take notice of his hopeless, homeless, and poisoned life.

VERSE 20

Surely my soul remembers / and is bowed down within me

The word *remember* here is repeated as if the prayer for God to remember has now caused Jeremiah to remember as well. In essence, this verse reads, "Lord, remember my affliction, for surely I will never forget it. You have taught me lessons I will never forget." Some English translations give the impression that Jeremiah slips further into despair here: "I continually think about this, and I am depressed" (NET).

It may be, however, that the plea in verse 19 for God to remember began to shift Jeremiah's memory back to the truth of God's Word, as verses 21 and on indicate. Thus he did indeed remember his own poverty, homelessness, and poisoned life, but now his "soul" is "laid low" as he repents and intercedes on behalf of Judah. Any arrogance of soul was knocked out of Jeremiah.[1] He was

---

1   R. Laird Harris, editor, *Theological Wordbook of the Old Testament* (Chicago: Moody Press, 1980).

humbled before God. Here then, Jeremiah confesses that his soul was humbled, and the following context reveals his submissive faith in God.

VERSE 21

This I recall to my mind, therefore I have hope

Jeremiah literally wrote: "This I turn back to my heart, therefore I have hope." In asking Yahweh to "remember," Jeremiah was prompted by the Spirit of God to "turn back" or "restore" the rightful place of the Word of God in His thinking. Despite the destruction around him, Jeremiah obtains hope by changing his focus. He looks *away* from the desolation of the city and *toward* the character of Yahweh, as revealed in His Word.

Because the poet has turned his heart back to the truth of God's Word and His mercy and faithfulness, he has hope. The word here translated "hope" involves a patient waiting for and anticipation of God's intervention (cf. 2 Kings 6:33 for the exact form of the same word translated "wait"; see the same root in Psalm 119:43, 49, 74, 81, 114, 147; 130:5; 147:11). Job 13:15 echoes the poet's thought here: "Though he slay me, yet will I hope in Him." The KJV translates the word *hope* as "trust": "Though he slay me, yet will I trust in Him."

Hope returns when the sufferer turns his heart back to the truth of the Word of God and the faithful character of God. And that turning of heart—a change of mind, repentance—is followed by taking refuge in the unfailing love, mercy, and compassion of Yahweh.

VERSE 22

The LORD's lovingkindnesses indeed never cease

The plural form of the Hebrew word *chesed* is the first word of this verse followed by *Yahweh*. Jeremiah's hope found a sure foundation—the lovingkindnesses of Yahweh. *Chesed*, or lovingkindness, used 250 times in the Old Testament, is almost untranslatable to English— it carries various nuances of "loyal love," "faithful mercy," "unfailing love," and "kindness." It is perhaps the Old Testament equivalent to the New Testament concept of grace. The prophet chooses to shift his focus *away* from Judah's sin and its consequences and instead look *toward* the grace of God.

Jeremiah turned his heart back from self, and a very distant view of God's sovereign chastening (vv. 1–18), to "Yahweh"—the covenant keeping God of Israel and His loyal, unfailing, faithful mercies, kindness, love, and grace. This renewed perspective then fuels him to praise God in the midst of affliction.

The phrase translated "indeed never cease" is literally "that we are not finished." The KJV renders the verse: "It is of the LORD's mercies that we are not consumed." Both translations are theologically accurate and grammatically possible within a poetic context. God's gracious, loyal, and unfailing love is never finished, and because of it, we are not finished or consumed. Nehemiah would recognize this after Jeremiah's day, perhaps in part because of this verse (cf. Nehemiah 9:31; see also Malachi 3:6). The grammar, however, favors the translation that "it is because of Yahweh's lovingkindnesses that we are not consumed."

For His compassions never fail

Using poetic parallelism, Jeremiah says, "For His tender compassions never fail." *Compassions* is related to the word for "womb" and communicates a tender care and affection. *Fail* here is a synonym for *cease* and also speaks of being finished. Yahweh's grace and tender care never come to an end. Perhaps Jeremiah remembered the words of Micah 7:18–20 (see also Psalm 77:6–11; Isaiah 49:15). "God's compassion towards his children does not come to an end no matter how severely he acts against their sin."[2]

VERSE 23

They are new every morning

God's "tender mercies" are "new every morning." This is evident with each day of creation in Genesis 1. The promise God made after the flood testifies to His faithful Word and tender mercies each morning, as He said in Genesis 8:22: "While the earth remains, seedtime and harvest, and cold and heat, and summer and winter, and day and night shall not cease." The provision of manna every day for forty years in the wilderness also demonstrates God's faithful mercies (Exodus 16:35; cf. Nehemiah 9:20–21).

---

2   John L. Mackay, *Lamentations: A Mentor Commentary* (Fearn: Christian Focus, 2008), 141.

After enumerating his despair (vv. 1–18), Jeremiah's poem turns to *remembering the truth* (vv. 19–23a), which in turn leads to renewed worship.

Great is Your faithfulness

Here Jeremiah turns to direct worship, affirming God's trustworthy character. The word *faithfulness* refers to steadfastness, firmness, and fidelity.[3] It is from the same root as the word *amen*. Jeremiah cries out, "Great is Your utter dependability. The Lord alone is ever true." The prophet worshiped Yahweh by affirming His Word back to Him. Psalm 36:5–7 says: "Your lovingkindness, O LORD, extends to the heavens, Your faithfulness reaches to the skies. Your righteousness is like the mountains of God; Your judgments are like a great deep. O LORD, You preserve man and beast. How precious is Your lovingkindness, O God! And the children of men take refuge in the shadow of Your wings" (see also Psalm 40:10–11; 89:1–2; 119:90).

VERSE 24

"The LORD is my portion," says my soul, "Therefore I have hope in Him"

In verse 17, while spiraling downward toward despair, the poet wrote: "My soul has been rejected from peace." In verse 20, he said: "Remembering, my soul remembers and is bowed low within me." Now Jeremiah confidently affirms that not only is God merciful and faithful, but He is also sufficient.

Portion can speak of an allotment or inheritance (cf. Numbers 18:20). Psalm 16:5–6 says, "The LORD is the portion of my inheritance and my cup; You support my lot. The lines have fallen to me in pleasant places; indeed, my heritage is beautiful to me." The same term is used in Ecclesiastes 2:10, there translated "reward" (see also Psalm 119:57; 142:5). As Psalm 73:26 says, "My flesh and my heart may fail, but God is the strength of my heart and my portion forever." After turning from self-focus and humbly remembering the truth of God's Word and Yahweh's character, Jeremiah becomes satisfied with Yahweh alone. God is enough, as the psalmist writes, "The LORD is my shepherd, I shall not [be in] want [of any good thing]" (Psalm 23:1). He is the prophet's security and inheritance.

---

3 Francis Brown, *Enhanced Brown-Driver-Briggs Hebrew and English Lexicon* (Oxford: Clarendon Press, 1906).

Recognizing the sufficiency of the Lord leads the prophet to place his hope completely in Him. Verses 21 and 24 are like bookends. "This I recall to my mind, therefore I have hope" and "The Lord is my portion…therefore I have hope in Him." Where is hope found? It is found in Him. Hope is found in the Lord Himself—in His character, nature, and faithfulness.

VERSE 25

The Lord is good to those who wait for Him, to the person who seeks Him

The prophet ventures to use the divine name Yahweh three times in three verses after declaring His faithfulness (vv. 24–26). The truth of God's Word flooded back to Jeremiah's mind as he wrote of what is "good" in verses 25–27. Each verse begins with the Hebrew word for "good." First, "Good is Yahweh, to those who wait for Him." This truth is revealed throughout the Scriptures and is the focus of many of the Psalms (see for example Psalm 25:8–10; 27:14; 37:7–11, 34; 40:1–5; 62:1–2, 5–8; 86:5; 130:5–8; cf. Genesis 48:18; Isaiah 40:31; 64:4; Micah 7:7–8; Nahum 1:7; see also Jeremiah 29:10–14).

The second half of the verse reveals what it means to wait for the Lord. To "wait" is not to be idle in one's thoughts or activities until He shows up, but rather to seek Him. The exact form of the word *seek* was also used in Deuteronomy 4:29 in a prophetic context that at least initially applied to Jeremiah's day (cf. also 1 Chronicles 28:9). As the writer of Hebrews said some six hundred years later: "Now faith is the assurance of things hoped for, the conviction of things not seen.… And without faith it is impossible to please [God], for he who comes to God must believe that He is and that He is a rewarder of those who seek Him" (Hebrews 1:1, 6). Psalm 9:10 says, "And those who know Your name will put their trust in You, for You, O Lord, have not forsaken those who seek You" (see also Psalm 119:2; Isaiah 55:6–7).

VERSE 26

It is good that he waits silently for the salvation of the Lord

It is "good" for the sufferer who seeks God in faith to wait silently for the salvation of Yahweh. *Silently* seems to indicate a quiet trust that is not constantly thinking or speaking of other avenues of deliverance besides the Lord. Isaiah

30:15–16a says, "For thus the Lord God, the Holy One of Israel, has said, 'In repentance and rest you will be saved, *in quietness and trust is your strength.*' But you were not willing, and you said, 'No, for we will flee on horses.'" In other words, it is best that the believer cultivates longsuffering.

Verse 27

It is good for a man that he should / bear the yoke in his youth

As in 3:1, the term "man" here is *geber.* The yoke in this context may be speaking specifically of the burden of the consequences of sin (1:14; cf. Deuteronomy 28:48) or perhaps hardship in general. *Youth* does not necessarily refer to childhood only, but the time of strength and vitality, much as Ecclesiastes 12:1 says: "Remember also your Creator in the days of your youth, before the evil days come and the years draw near when you will say, 'I have no delight in them.'" The thought seems to be parallel to the instruction found in Hebrews 12:5–11. Jeremiah had certainly suffered the consequences of others' sins as a "youth" (see Jeremiah 1:7–8). And perhaps now he saw how those early days of divine discipline had prepared him to weather the storm of this calamity. He has learned that it's best that we submit to the Lord early on, without procrastination, without waiting until times of painful correction come. As Romans 5:3–4: "We also exult in our tribulations, knowing that tribulation brings about perseverance; and perseverance, proven character; and proven character, hope."

Verse 28

Let him sit alone and be silent / since He has laid it on him

Silent here intimates faith and a stillness or rest. Psalm 37:7 says, "Rest [same root as *silent*] in the Lord and wait patently for Him; do not fret because of him who prospers in his way, because of the man who carries out wicked schemes" (cf. again Psalm 62:5–8). And Psalm 131:2 illustrates this type of *stillness*: "Surely I have composed and quieted [same root as *silent*] my soul; like a weaned child rests against his mother, my soul is like a weaned child within me."

Jeremiah is advocating a submissive heart under God's discipline. He is saying, "Let him who is afflicted silently accept God's discipline without complaining or accusing God of unfair treatment." The call to "sit alone" indicates that those experiencing God's discipline are not to seek their comfort in anyone else other than God Himself.

VERSE 29

Let him put his mouth in the dust

Jeremiah now has a different perspective than he did in 3:16. Here he is calling for a willing acceptance of humiliation with one's "mouth in the dust." This is repentance—a true change of mind—concerning one's circumstances.

Perhaps there is hope

The "perhaps" here does not so much imply doubt as it indicates humility. The idea is much like the king of Nineveh's proclamation after Jonah had preached destruction: "Both man and beast must be covered with sackcloth; and let men call on God earnestly that each may turn from his wicked way and from the violence which is in his hands. *Who knows* [perhaps], God may turn and relent and withdraw His burning anger so that we will not perish" (Jonah 3:8). This idea is seen also in Jesus' account of the prodigal son (Luke 15) and the parable of the publican and the Pharisee (Luke 18:13). The thought is, *Though I know I deserve this, since God is compassionate, He may well have mercy and lift my mouth from the dust.*

VERSE 30

Let him give his cheek to the smiter, let him be filled with reproach

It's one thing to quietly wait for God's deliverance—and even accept humiliation by voluntarily bowing down in the midst of one's circumstances—but it is even more difficult for a man to "give his cheek to the smiter." That is, "Let him submit to the means of God's discipline. Let him peacefully submit to the heavenly spanking. Let him receive the correction that God brings." Job knew this reproach as well, and the wording is strikingly similar to Jeremiah's here: "They have gaped at me with their mouth, they have slapped me on the cheek with contempt, they have massed themselves against me" (Job 16:10). Micah 5:1 also has similar imagery in the context of messianic hope: "Now muster yourselves in troops, daughter of troops; they have laid siege against us; with a rod they will smite the judge of Israel on the cheek" (note, though, that the Lord will not reject forever according to Micah 5:2ff). Perhaps Jeremiah remembered the prophecy concerning the coming Servant-Redeemer in Isaiah 50:6–7: "I gave My back to those who strike Me, and My cheeks to those who pluck out the beard; I did not cover My face from humiliation and spitting. For the Lord God helps Me, therefore, I am not disgraced; therefore, I have set My face like flint, and I know that I will not be ashamed."

VERSE 31

For the Lord will not reject forever

The prophet went on to write that the Sovereign Master, Adonai, "will not reject forever." Again the language is strikingly similar to Psalm 77:7 (note the context of hopelessness turning to hope). Psalm 94:14 says, "For the LORD will not abandon His people, nor will He forsake His inheritance." Jeremiah also had the promises of restoration given to Isaiah and in his own writings (Isaiah 54:7–10; Jeremiah 31:31–40; 32:40; 33:14–26; Micah 7:18–20). This is not just wishful thinking, but truth revealed by God. Suffering will come to an end; God will not reject His children in the midst of their suffering even though they may feel He has.

VERSE 32

For if He causes grief / then He will have compassion / according to His abundant lovingkindness

Echoing verse 22, Jeremiah again speaks of God's tender care and loyal love. According to 1:5, He had indeed caused Israel "grief" because of the multitude of her iniquities. But God did not discipline her and then cast her away from Himself. He chastened her and then pulled her close to assure her. See this theme of God's "compassion" in Exodus 2:23–25; 3:7; Judges 10:16; 2 Kings 13:23; Psalm 103:11–13; 106:43–45; Jeremiah 31:15–20. Isaiah 54:8 says, "'In an outburst of anger I hid My face from you for a moment, but with everlasting lovingkindness I will have compassion on you,' says the LORD your Redeemer." Again, remember the father's response to the prodigal: "But while he was still a long way off, his father saw him and felt compassion for him, and ran and embraced him and kissed him" (Luke 15:20). In essence, Yahweh is saying, "I want you to remember that I love you. I am bringing this pain and suffering into your life because I want the best for you, because I want to change you. Therefore, submit to Me and you will learn and grow."

VERSE 33

For He does not afflict willingly / or grieve the sons of men
Literally, the Hebrew here reads: "For He does not afflict from His heart or grieve the sons of men." God does not take pleasure in the pain of others, or the death of the wicked (Ezekiel 18:32; 33:11). He does not delight in grieving others. But His goodness certainly calls Him to punish iniquity. He is not One who simply gets angry and then takes it out on us. He loves us enough to draw us close through discipline so that we are corrected. Charles Dyer writes, "Judah's afflictions were not cruel acts of a capricious God who delighted in inflicting pain on helpless people. Rather the afflictions came from a compassionate God who was being faithful to His covenant. He did not enjoy making others suffer, but He allowed the afflictions as temporary means to force Judah back to Himself."[4]

The psalmist wrote in Psalm 119:75–77a: "I know, O LORD, that Your judgments are righteous, and that in faithfulness You have afflicted me. O may Your lovingkindness comfort me, according to Your word to Your servant. May Your compassion come to me that I may live...."

VERSE 34

To crush under His feet / all the prisoners of the land
Verses 34–36 form one sentence in the Hebrew. *Prisoners* likely refers to war captives.[5] The pronoun *His* here may refer to an oppressor, rather than to God. The NLT translates this verse: "If people crush under foot all the prisoners of the land."

The end of the sentence found in verse 36 makes it clear that the Sovereign

---

4   Charles Dyer, "Lamentations" in John F. Walvoord and Roy B. Zuck, eds., *The Bible Knowledge Commentary* (Wheaton: Victor Books, 1985), 1218.
5   Walter C. Kaiser, *Grief and Pain in the Plan of God* (Fearn: Christian Focus, 2004), 92.

Master does not approve of oppression and bondage. He approves of justice and disapproves of the neglect of it. "For the LORD loves justice and does not forsake His godly ones; they are preserved forever, but the descendants of the wicked will be cut off" (Psalm 37:28). Isaiah 51:22–23 also clearly reveals this point:

> Thus says the Lord, the LORD, even your God who contends for His people, 'Behold, I have taken out of your hand the cup of reeling, the chalice of My anger. You will never drink it again. I will put it into the hand of your tormentors, who have said to you, "Lie down that we may walk over you." You have even made your back like the ground and like the street for those who walk over it.

VERSE 35

To deprive a man of justice in the presence of the Most High

The Hebrew term here translated "deprive" is used in Proverbs 17:23 to convey a similar truth: "A wicked man receives a bribe from the bosom to *pervert* [same word] the ways of justice." Proverbs 18:5 says, "To show partiality to the wicked is not good, nor to *thrust aside* [same word] the righteous in judgment" (see also Isaiah 10:2).

"In the presence of the Most High," or literally, "Before the face of the Most High," reveals that the "Most High," the exalted and omnipotent One, is also the omniscient One. He sees and will deal with all perversions of justice.

VERSE 36

To defraud a man in his lawsuit

Defraud means to "cheat" (Amos 8:5). It refers to that which is "twisted" or "bent." This verse indicates that God did not approve of the defrauding by means of lawsuit taking place among the people of Israel. This grievous practice is also rebuked in the New Testament (1 Corinthians 6:1–8). See Deuteronomy 16:19; 24:17; 27:19 for the same concept.

Of these things the Lord does not approve

Oppression and injustice never go unpunished in God's economy. "Of these things *Adonai* does not look upon [with approval]."[6] See also Habakkuk 1:13.

VERSE 37

Who is there who speaks and it comes to pass, unless the Lord has commanded?

Jeremiah reassures the people that all suffering is regulated by the absolute sovereignty of God. Again he uses the term *Adonai*, Sovereign Master, to reference God. The sense is that no one can speak without his speech somehow working toward God's sovereign end. Psalm 33:9–11 says, "For He spoke, and it was done; He commanded, and it stood fast. The LORD nullifies the counsel of the nations; He frustrates the plans of the peoples. The counsel of the LORD stands forever, the plans of His heart from generation to generation." Jeremiah himself wrote: "I know, O LORD, that a man's way is not in himself, nor is it in a man who walks to direct his steps" (Jeremiah 10:23). See Proverbs 16:1, 4, 9, 33; 19:21; 20:24; 21:30–31; Isaiah 46:8–11.

VERSE 38

Is it not from the mouth of the Most High / that both good and ill go forth?

Some may question if God is sovereign over calamities in the world, even the evil perpetrated by evil men. This statement addresses this question directly: The One who is exalted as "Most High" over all things is sovereign over "both good and ill" (literally "the evil and the good"). Perhaps Jeremiah was thinking of the narrative in Job 1:12 and 2:6, where the Lord allowed Satan to bring calamity upon Job. And Job seemed to understand the sovereignty of God when he said, "Shall we indeed accept good from God and not accept adversity?" (Job 2:10).

The Scriptures do not teach that God is evil or the cause of evil, but the Bible does portray Him as using both good and ill for His good purposes. This is the mystery of absolute sovereignty. Like Jeremiah's assertion here, the prophet

---

6 See discussion in Mackay, 152.

Isaiah boldly spoke on the Lord's behalf when he said: "The One forming light and creating darkness, causing well-being and creating calamity; I am the LORD who does all these" (Isaiah 45:7). Joseph understood that what men mean for evil God uses for good; he confidently asserted that even their evil was used by God to accomplish His good purpose (Genesis 50:20).

VERSE 39

Why should any living mortal, or any man offer complaint in view of his sins?

Complaint is used elsewhere only in Numbers 11:1. It refers to a continual sighing (YLT). In other words, mortal man has no right to complain against God for the suffering his own sin has brought upon him. Proverbs 19:3 is quite instructive on how men complain against God because of the consequences of their own sin: "The foolishness of man ruins his way, and his heart rages against the LORD." It may be that Jeremiah was making the point that they had survived and thus were actually recipients of a certain amount of divine favor. The survivors were sinners too, yet they had been spared—to complain would betray a self-imposed blindness to God's mercy. He says in effect, "Remember what you really deserve in light of your sins, and there is reason for hope."

INSIGHTS FOR COUNSELING

It may be instructive to trace the heart attitude of the prophet up to this point in the third chapter. Jeremiah's honesty and humility in the face of God's chastening become evident as he extensively describes God's discipline. God's hand of blessing has turned into a fist of wrath (vv. 1–3); His healing touch has brought hardship (vv. 4–6); His hearing ear has become a silent prison (vv. 7–9); His fellowship has turned into hostility (vv. 10–12); His acceptance has been replaced by rejection (vv. 13–15); and His peace has turned into fear and despair (vv. 16–18). Jeremiah's humility is also evident in his response to God's discipline (vv. 19–20).

But then the turning point! In verses 21–23, Jeremiah remembers the mercy and faithfulness of God: "This I recall to my mind, therefore I have hope. The LORD's lovingkindnesses indeed never cease, for His compassions never fail.

They are new every morning; great is Your faithfulness." In the midst of Judah's affliction, Jeremiah chooses to turn his eyes from their suffering to the Lord. He chooses to refocus. He chooses to remember truths about God that are rock-solid foundation stones—His mercy, faithfulness, and compassion.

This is the key to responding to suffering in a manner that pleases the Lord. The Bible reveals the spiritual profit that comes to us by means of the Lord's discipline. For example, King Solomon writes, "My son, do not reject the discipline of the LORD or loathe His reproof, for whom the LORD loves He reproves, even as a father corrects the son in whom he delights" (Proverbs 3:11–12). Discipline is a mark of the love of God. Proverbs 6:23 also affirms, "For the commandment is a lamp and the teaching is light; and reproofs for discipline are the way of life." Reproofs for discipline are the way of life, the way to live, the way to life.

Since this is true, we should always respond to the Lord's chastening in a teachable manner, asking, "Lord, what am I to learn from this?" or, "What are You aiming to change in me?" Whether our suffering is caused by deliberate acts of sin or the natural consequences of living in a sin-cursed world, our priority must be to look to the Lord as our only hope and our all-sufficient portion.

Too often we place our hope in the thought that things will get better, making a habit of getting through each affliction by mustering up enough confidence to say to ourselves, "Things will get better. Someday this trial will be over. It will be better tomorrow or next year or the year after that." However, that is not necessarily true. It may not get better until we see the Lord face-to-face. And we must accept that. If we place our hope in the possibility that things will get better tomorrow, we are placing our hope in that which may very well fail. But God will not fail. God's mercy and faithfulness will endure while He chastens His people. In light of this confidence, we must take time to dwell on numerous biblical principles.

1. Submission is the right response to discipline.

Too often we flee from God's discipline instead of submitting and saying, "Lord, this discipline, though painful, is good for me and I know I will be trained by it. Therefore, I submit." If you habitually run from painful experiences, you will never grow. If you refuse to submit to His rod of discipline, you will spend your entire life as a spiritual toddler, running from God's spankings. But God wants us to grow up. Therefore, we must discipline ourselves to face our sin with honesty and humility. Jeremiah's prescription for hope in the face of adversity begins with remembering that the Lord is good to those who wait for and seek Him (Lamentations 3:25). But waiting for the Lord's salvation means receiving the Lord's chastening rather than fighting against it (vv. 28–30).

2. When we are suffering under the chastening of God, we must remember His mercy and faithfulness.

You will find no hope in your circumstances. You will find no hope in wishing things will get better. You will find no hope in wishing the pain will go away or in trumped-up optimism. Nor is hope found in other people. But hope is in God! You will find hope only if you turn your focus away from the destruction, away from the desolation, away from the pain and look to the character of God—because He will never fail you. God is merciful; He is faithful. Hope in God (Lamentations 3:21–23; Psalm 42:1–11).

3. Endurance under discipline is supplied by God Himself.

Each day we receive a fresh supply of mercy, love, and grace for whatever trials that day may hold. Consideration of the sum of His great faithfulness is critical to sustaining faith. Remember that the Lord's compassion and abundant grace will outweigh any affliction you may suffer (Lamentations 3:23–24; 2 Corinthians 12:9).

4. In times of affliction, we must resist the temptation to resort to self-pity.

We get our eyes off the Lord. We get trapped into thinking only of our sins or the ways others have sinned against us, and by doing so, we live in the past, unable to move forward. Here Jeremiah sets a pattern for us: Take it to the Lord in prayer. Get your eyes off yourself, your circumstances, or how poorly you have been treated. Depression and despair can sometimes be symptoms of an arrogant heart that places self at the center of the universe. When self's expectations repeatedly aren't met, such arrogance turns to sullen anger or perhaps somber emotionlessness that defies submission and humility before God. Proverbs 3:34 says that God "gives grace to the afflicted." Look to God and trust that He is indeed the One who will never fail you (Lamentations 3:19–20, Psalm 27:10; Hebrews 13:5).

5. Waiting on the Lord is not passive.

To wait on the Lord means to seek Him, to actively obey Him while resting in Him to accomplish His will in the midst of our affliction. So when we find ourselves in the darkened valley of suffering, we need to wait on Him by seeking Him. That means we must obey Him, trust Him, and respond with a teachable spirit. We see this same principle in Isaiah 40:29–31: "He gives strength to the weary, and to him who lacks might He increases power. Though youths grow weary and tired, and vigorous young men stumble badly, yet those who wait for the LORD will gain new strength; they will mount up with wings like eagles, they will run and not get tired, they will walk and not become weary." Those who wait for the Lord receive new strength for their times of weariness. We shouldn't delay seeking the Lord, waiting until times of correction come. It is good to wait on the Lord by submitting to Him in our youth. Don't procrastinate. Don't wait until you are drowning in the deep waters of suffering to cry out to Him. Seek Him now (Lamentations 3:25–26).

6. Deliberately focusing our mind on the truth of God's Word is not a mind trick, but rather an essential Christian discipline.

Walter Kaiser has aptly written concerning what some might call a psychological ploy of mind over matter, or positive thinking that denies reality: "Was this some kind of mental gymnastics in which the mind was placed above and beyond the matters at hand? Should afflicted people deny themselves all expression of tears and lamentation? On the contrary, every line so far in this book has urged us to work through our grief in part by expressing it from a to z."[7] Jeremiah renewed His worship by remembering and directly affirming back to God His trustworthy and true character (Lamentations 3:21–23).

7. The soul that finds its satisfaction in the Lord alone will wait patiently in hope for His deliverance.

Faith and hope are found in the midst of desperate circumstances as we remember the truth of God's Word and God's character, which leads to a renewal of worship and reaffirmation of satisfaction in the LORD alone. This is how the believer claims and proclaims his trust in Yahweh's character no matter the circumstances (Lamentations 3:24; Romans 8:24–25).

---

7   Kaiser, 89.

8. God's sovereignty is one of the most comforting truths revealed in Scripture.

Most Christians find it easy to say, "I believe that God is sovereign over all the good things that happen to me," but not many testify the same about the evil things that happen to them. Instead they apparently believe that God stepped off His throne momentarily and everything turned to chaos. But how would we like to trust a God who does not know about tomorrow? Jeremiah writes "Is it not from the mouth of the Most High that both good and ill go forth?" (Lamentations 3:38). Somehow, in the mysterious plan of God, all of the evil things that occur in our lives work together for His good end (Romans 8:28).

If we are struggling with this concept, we need only remember Joseph, a man sold into slavery by his own blood brothers, falsely accused by a loose woman, and thrown into prison and forgotten by those he helped—*but remembered by God*. Many years later, when reunited with his family, Joseph's brothers feared that he would treat them the same way they had treated him. However, Joseph responded with an amazing statement. As he looked into his brothers' eyes, he said, "As for you, you meant evil against me, but God meant it for good in order to bring about this present result, to preserve many people alive" (Genesis 50:20). God had raised Joseph to the second most powerful position in Egypt in order to save His chosen nation from the famine and thus preserve the earthly line of the Messiah, Jesus Christ.

God had a good plan in mind all along. We also must trust that somehow He is bringing good to pass through the trouble we experience. In this life, the good that will be accomplished is the shaping of our heart and life into the image of Christ (Romans 8:29). Beyond this, we cannot fully know the details of God's plan. That is why we walk by faith and not by sight (Lamentations 3:37–38; 2 Corinthians 5:7).

9. A tragedy occurs when believers take each other to court to solve their squabbles, because the name of God is blasphemed before the watching world.

Instead of being willing to be defrauded, Christians in the church at Corinth were willing to defraud fellow believers in Christ. No wonder Paul writes this "to [their] shame" (1 Corinthians 6:1–8). Like Jeremiah and Paul, we need to support what God approves and reject what God disapproves (Lamentations 3:36).

10. When God chastens us, He does not enjoy making us suffer but appoints suffering as a temporary means of drawing us back to Him.

The reason for this is that God knows the end of sin, but we do not. We see only the pleasures of sin rather than its ultimate outcome. But God cares enough to correct us so that we do not completely destroy ourselves and our families. He is like the parent who grabs his child and pulls him out of the path of the oncoming truck. He knows the end result of our foolishness. He does not simply stand back and watch us get run over by a truckload of sin. Instead, He stops us in order to correct us so that we may learn to live within His boundaries, which is the place where His blessing abounds. As we have already been reminded of numerous times, "All discipline for the moment seems not to be joyful, but sorrowful; yet to those who have been trained by it, afterwards it yields the peaceful fruit of righteousness" (Hebrews 12:11). Like Jeremiah, we need to learn to submit to God's discipline and be trained in His righteousness. God loves us too much to let us remain in our old ways (Lamentations 3:32–33).

Homework for Counseling

You are encouraged to photocopy homework pages for use in personal counseling.

Part 1: Shifting Your Focus

1. Make a list of the attributes and works of God that display His faithfulness in your life. Using these truths, write out a prayer of praise to God.
2. Make a list of the forms of divine discipline present in your current circumstances.
    - How are you seeking God in your chastening?
    - In what ways are you submitting to His discipline?
    - In what ways are you resisting it?
    - What does your response to discipline say about your faith in the sovereignty of God?
3. Read Psalm 38. Notice David's reverent honesty as he pours out his heart to God. List every expression of David that reveals his inner turmoil. Pray this psalm back to God, confessing sins, crying out for help, and thanking God for His kindness and forgiveness.

PART 2: HOPING IN JESUS

God's promise to those who know Him through repentant faith in Jesus Christ is that He will never reject us. Jesus says, "I will never desert you, nor will I ever forsake you" (Hebrews 13:5). God will reject unbelievers forever, but He will not reject His children. He will not reject those who trust in Christ since we are accepted in Him. When God disciplines us He does not place His grace and mercy aside. Instead, He dispenses His love, mercy, and grace *as* He disciplines us. If He did not do this, we would be consumed or cast away forever.

Therefore, like Jeremiah, we need to surrender to the Lord's sovereignty. We do this by surrendering to the Lord Jesus. Acts 10:42 says that God has appointed Jesus as "judge of the living and the dead." Jesus will judge all sin righteously. For believers, God has already judged our sin in Christ. If you are truly born again by the power of the gospel, your sin has already been righteously judged by God in the body of Jesus on the Cross of Calvary.

But perhaps you are not a believer, but rather are content to play the game called *church*. Perhaps your parents are Christians and you think that simply being related to them automatically makes you a Christian, but you are not truly born again. You don't have different desires; you still have the same desires as your unbelieving friends. You are fooling yourself. Your sins have not been righteously taken care of. If you die in that state, those sins will be righteously taken care of when God rejects you forever. So God's invitation to you is the same: Come to Christ; be forgiven. Come to Jesus; find mercy with Him.

God offers us His mercy because His Son has absorbed the Father's wrath against our sin. "He made Him who knew no sin to be sin on our behalf, so that we might become the righteousness of God in Him" (2 Corinthians 5:21). God treated Jesus the way a sinner deserves to be treated so that sinners like us could receive His righteousness by faith. "He Himself bore our sins in His body on the cross, so that we might die to sin and live to righteousness" (1 Peter 2:24). Do you trust this Jesus? Or are you trusting in yourself or your own moral reform? God is rich in mercy (Ephesians 2:4), mercy that is found only in Jesus Christ. Come to Him today.

1. Memorize Lamentations 3:24-25.
2. List the ways in which you are genuinely seeking Christ. Is there any-thing or anyone else that you are looking to provide for you security and satisfaction?

Chapter 5

"Let Us Return to the Lord"

The Supplication of Repentance and Faith

Lamentations 3:40–66

Jerusalem is destroyed. The city is in ruins. The temple has been leveled. Why? Because of Judah's sin. "I am the man who has seen affliction," writes Jeremiah, "because of the rod of His wrath" (Lamentations 3:1). Through the faithful preaching of Jeremiah, the people of God now realize that their own rebellion is the cause of their suffering, and they have moved to embrace the loyal love and tender mercies of God in the aftermath of His discipline. So what do they do now? The answer comes from God through the mouth of His prophet: "Repent of your sin and return to Me in faith."

There must be sustained repentance and a determined faith that abides—or else self-focus and despondency may reappear and consume them again. The last section of Lamentations 3 reveals the repentance and tenacious faith that sets believers on the road to ongoing victory over despair. Like Jeremiah and Judah, we must repent of our sin and return to the Lord. We must be honest before the Lord, confess our sins, and call upon Him in faith in order to be restored to God.

In Lamentations 3:40–66, we see four movements in Jeremiah's supplication of repentance and faith that will help us submit to and thrive under the sure discipline of God without wavering.

TEACHING OUTLINES

Option A

Seeking God in the Wake of Sin's Misery

  I.   A song of sorrow and despair (1:1–22)
 II.   A song of sovereignty and divine discipline (2:1–22)
III.   A song of suffering and determination/dependence/hope (3:1–66)

    A. The suffering of the servant enumerated [The man of sorrows] (3:1–18)

    B. The steadfast love of the LORD embraced [The LORD of hope] (3:19–39)

    C. The supplication of repentance and faith expressed [The prayer of dependence/faith] (3:40–66)

      1. The call to repentance (v. 40)

      2. The confession of sin (vv. 41–42)

        a. Turning to God (v. 41)

        b. Telling the truth (v. 42)

      3. The consequences of sin (vv. 43–47)

        a. Divine anger (vv. 43–44)

          i. The pursuit and execution of judgment (v. 43)

          ii. The prayer than cannot penetrate (v. 44)

        b. Devastation and destruction (vv. 45–47)

          i. Rejection (v. 45)

          ii. Ridicule (v. 46)

          iii. Ruin (v. 47)

      4. The confirmation of faith (vv. 48–66)

        a. The tenacity of faith in the mercy of the LORD (vv. 48–51)

          i. Tears due to the destruction (v. 48)

          ii. Tenacity in seeking the mercy and compassion of Yahweh (vv. 49–50)

          iii. Torture in seeing the consequences of sin (v. 51)

        b. The testing of faith in desperate circumstances (vv. 52–54)

          i. The prey of hunters (v. 52)

   ii. The pit of silence (v. 53)

   iii. The plunge beneath the waters of death (v. 54)

  c. The triumph of faith in assurance of salvation (vv. 55–58)

   i. The call of faith to Yahweh (v. 55)

   ii. The compassion of Yahweh (v. 56)

   iii. The comfort of Yahweh (v. 57)

   iv. The confidence of sovereign redemption (v. 58)

  d. The trust of faith—that the LORD sees and will repay (vv. 59–66)

   i. The LORD sees (vv. 59–60)

    aa. He has seen my oppression (v. 59)

    bb. He has seen their opposition (v. 60)

   ii. The LORD hears (vv. 61–62)

    aa. He has heard their reproach (v. 61)

    bb. He has heard their whispering (v. 62)

   iii. The LORD is faithful to His promises (vv. 63–66)

    aa. The call of the afflicted (v. 63)

    bb. The confidence of justice (v. 64)

    cc. The covenant promises (vv. 65–66; cf. Deuteronomy 30:7)

Option B

 I. The call to repentance (vv. 40–41)

 II. The confession of sin (vv. 42–47)

 III. The crying of the prophet (vv. 48–51)

 IV. The condition of the oppressed (vv. 52–54)

 V. The call for help (vv. 55–66)

  A. God heard him and drew near (vv. 55–58)

  B. God took vengeance on the prophet's enemies (vv. 59–66)

EXPOSITION
VERSE 40

Let us examine and probe our ways, and let us return to the LORD

The proper response to Judah's affliction is repentance—they must return to the Lord. Notably, Jeremiah turns back to the first person plural pronoun *us*. *Examine* and *probe* both speak of an intense search (cf. Proverbs 2:4). The prophet is calling the survivors to consider the many ways they have rebelled against God and disobeyed His Word and to return to Him in faith. In 5:21, the word *return* is translated "renew." See Deuteronomy 30:1–10, which follows the covenant curses, and note the hope offered to those who "return to the LORD" (see also 1 Kings 8:35–36, 47–50; 2 Chronicles 6:36–39; 7:13ff). Isaiah 55:7 says, "Let the wicked forsake his way and the unrighteous man his thoughts; and let him return to the LORD, and He will have compassion on him, and to our God, for He will abundantly pardon."

Jeremiah's poem turns from a personal embrace of Yahweh's steadfast love to a corporate call for self-examination and repentance—a renewed relationship with the covenant-keeping God, Yahweh.

VERSE 41

We lift up our heart and hands / toward God in heaven

Lift once again can be translated as an exhortation: "Let us lift up our heart and hands toward God in heaven." The call is not for merely an external act of prayer, lifting the palms upward, but a lifting of the entire inner man, the heart "toward God in heaven."

Much like the psalmist said in Psalm 139:23–24: "Search me, O God, and know my heart; try me and know my anxious thoughts; and see if there be any hurtful way in me, and lead me in the everlasting way." Psalm 86:4–5 says, "Make glad the soul of Your servant, for to You, O Lord, I lift up my soul. For you, Lord, are good, and ready to forgive, and abundant in lovingkindness to all who call upon You."

Repentance begins when self is examined in light of God's glory and truth—and an honest evaluation leads to the conclusion that one's heart is far from God. *To repent* means to return to a place of submission and obedience to the Lord by placing oneself under the authority of His Word. The call is to "lift up… heart and hands toward God in heaven." In verse 41 is an implicit confession that Israel's heart had been distanced from God. That is exactly the conclusion God wanted His people to come to; it was the purpose of the chastening He sent upon them. Moses had predicted:

> So it shall be when all of these things have come upon you, the blessing and the curse which I have set before you, and you call them to mind in all nations where the LORD your God has banished you, and you return to the LORD your God and obey Him with all your heart and soul according to all that I command you today, you and your sons, then the LORD your God will restore you from captivity, and have compassion on you, and will gather you again from all the peoples where the LORD your God has scattered you. (Deuteronomy 30:1–3)

The next verse explicitly confesses sin by affirming the truth about their past.

VERSE 42

We have transgressed and rebelled

The pronoun is emphatic: "We—we have transgressed and rebelled." The terms *transgressed* and *rebelled* emphasize the willful nature of Judah's rebellion. The NET Bible captures the thought as: "We have blatantly rebelled." Here the prophet displays the same pattern as other spiritual leaders in the Old Testament, such as Nehemiah and Daniel, both of whom confessed sin on behalf of their people (Nehemiah 1:6–7; Daniel 9:5–19). This confession parallels 1:18a: "The LORD is righteous; for I have rebelled against His command." In 5:16, Jeremiah writes: "Woe to us, for we have sinned." True faith involves self-examination in light of God's holiness, which leads to a turning to Him and telling the truth about one's sin. Note what the prophet had written on behalf of the LORD in Jeremiah 3:12–15. See also Daniel 9:5–19.

You have not pardoned

The contrast is also emphatic: "You—You have not pardoned." *We* on our part have knowingly and willfully rebelled. *You* on Your part have not forgiven. This is a startling acknowledgment of God's justice. For that moment in time, God withheld His forgiveness until they repented. God was unleashing His anger upon them as a nation, unwilling to pardon them until they met Him on His terms. This is an allusion to Deuteronomy 29:19–20:

> It shall be when he hears the words of this curse, that he will boast, saying, "I have peace though I walk in the stubbornness of my heart in order to destroy the watered land with the dry." The LORD shall never be willing to forgive him, but rather the anger of the LORD and His jealousy will burn against that man, and every curse which is written in this book will rest on him, and the LORD will blot out his name from under heaven.

God had spoken to Judah in Jeremiah 5:7, 9: "Why should I pardon you? Your sons have forsaken Me and sworn by those who are not gods. When I had fed them to the full, they committed adultery and trooped to the harlot's house.... 'Shall I not punish these people' declares the LORD, 'And on a nation such as this shall I not avenge Myself?'" (see also Ezekiel 24:13–14).

Jeremiah called the remnant to repentance and confessed Israel's sin and God's justice. In verses 43–47, the prophet details God's justice by chronicling, once again, some of the consequences of sin.

VERSE 43

You have covered Yourself with anger / and pursued us

With the use of the word *covered* here and in verse 44, Jeremiah is once again alluding to the divine chastening he had written of in similar language in 2:1: "How the Lord has covered the daughter of Zion with a cloud of His anger." Here, *Yourself* is supplied by the translators. But in verse 44 the pronoun is present. It is likely then that the imagery is of Judah being covered by Yahweh's judgment. Deuteronomy 28:45 also uses *pursued* in the context of divine judgment due to covenant unfaithfulness: "So all these curses shall come on you and pursue you and overtake you until you are destroyed, because you would not obey the LORD your God by keeping His commandments and His statutes which He commanded you" (cf. Lamentations 1:3, 6; see 3:66 for a reversal of divine pursuit).

Verses 43–47 all seem to reference back to the second chapter of Lamentations.

You have slain and have not spared

A more literal rendering would be: "You have killed—You have not pitied." Again this is reminiscent of 2:2, 17, 21. The prophet had predicted this in Jeremiah 13:14: "'I will dash them against each other, both the fathers and the sons together,' declares the LORD. 'I will not show pity nor be sorry nor have compassion so as not to destroy them'" (cf. also Ezra 7:9; 8:18; 9:10).

VERSE 44

You have covered yourself with a cloud / so that no prayer can pass through

Elsewhere in the Old Testament, Yahweh's presence was marked by a "cloud" that veiled His glory (Exodus 19:9; Numbers 12:5). But here His "cloud" signals divine opposition. Psalm 97:2 says, "Clouds and thick darkness surround Him; righteousness and justice are the foundation of His throne." Decades later, Zechariah the prophet would write: "'And just as He called and they would not listen, so they called and I would not listen,' says the LORD of hosts; 'but I scattered them with a storm wind among all the nations whom they have not known'" (Zechariah 7:13–14). This is another way of saying, "It is not Your problem, Lord. It is *our* problem. You are not answering our prayers, but not because You have changed. It is because we have rebelled and You have closed Your ears to us" (see also Jeremiah 14:11–12; 15:1; Psalm 80:4). Mackay makes an interesting observation: "Notice the difference in experience from 3:8, where the speaker felt his prayer never left the earth. Here it reaches heaven, only to find a 'Not available' notice on the door."[1]

Jeremiah once again writes of the consequences of sin—namely *divine anger*. In verses 45–47 he moves on to speak of devastation and destruction.

---

1   John L. Mackay, *Lamentations: A Mentor Commentary* (Fearn: Christian Focus, 2008), 159.

Verse 45

You have made us mere offscouring and refuse / in the midst of the peoples

Offscouring is used only here in the Scriptures. Some other English translations render it—"filth" (NRSV) or "scum" (NIV, ESV, NET). It refers to waste or sweepings—trash. The Holman Christian Standard Bible translates "offscouring and refuse" as "disgusting filth" (see also Lamentation 2:15).

Israel was like a sewer to the rest of the world. She had so wanted to embrace the world, but now she was disgusting to it because of the chastening of the LORD. Rejection is part of God's severe discipline. Because Israel did not want to be holy—set apart by God—but rather craved to be like every other nation, she worshipped the gods of this world. Then when she reaped the consequences of her sin, the world she so desperately loved turned its back on her. Pride is stripped away in the most painful way. Nahum 3:6 reveals a similar thought in a different context (dealing with Nineveh): "I will throw filth on you and make you vile, and set you up as a spectacle. And it will come about that all who see you will shrink from you." Deuteronomy 28:37 says: "You shall become a horror, a proverb, and a taunt among all the people where the LORD drives you."

Verse 46

All our enemies have opened their mouths against us

Again Jeremiah alludes to what was detailed in 2:16: "All your enemies have opened their mouths wide against you; they hiss and gnash their teeth" (see also Job 30:8–10; Psalm 22:6–8; 44:13–14; 79:4, 10).

Verse 47

Panic and pitfall have befallen us, devastation and destruction

The English here tries to capture the poetry of the Hebrew by using the alliterated doublets. The expression "panic and pit/pitfall" was also used in Isaiah

24:17 and Jeremiah 48:43. It pictures a panicked animal that unknowingly runs directly into a trap.[2]

The term *devastation* is rare, but the next phrase more fully describes Jeremiah's intent. *Destruction* is used in 1:15, translated "crush"; in 2:9, translated "broken"; in 2:11, translated "destruction"; in 2:13, translated "ruin"; and in 3:4, "broken." The destruction God brought upon Judah finally led the sinful nation to a true confession of their guilt. Now the people were ready to be reconciled to God and restored to a place of blessing. They finally understood why their lives were such a mess and why their city had been destroyed. It was because of their sin.

Jeremiah wrote this last portion of Lamentations 3 to model a prayer of repentance and faith. He begins with a *call to repentance* (v. 40); then he *confesses sin* (vv. 41–42); then he reviews *the consequences of sin* (vv. 43–47). Note that even after the spiritual epiphany of 3:21-26, the same temporal consequences remained. In verses 48–66, the prophet/songwriter turns once again to a more personal address and confirmation of faith.

VERSE 48

My eyes run down with streams of water / because of the destruction of the daughter of my people

As the poet once more employs first person singular pronouns (*I, me,* and *my*), this last portion of chapter 3 seems to answer the first 18 verses—this time with the perspective of faith and hope. Here Jeremiah's focus is once again on others, in compassionate weeping, rather than self-focus and distant despair. His grief is still a representative grief "because of the destruction of the daughter of my people [Jerusalem]."

As well, the allusions to chapter 2 continue in this third poem (cf. 2:11, 18). "Streams of water" were irrigation channels—his tears flowed unimpeded. Remember the prophet's words in Jeremiah 9:1: "Oh that my head were waters and my eyes a fountain of tears, that I might weep day and night for the slain of the daughter of my people" (cf. Jeremiah 13:17). Now the prophet was

---

2 Mackay, 160.

experiencing it. He was weeping in faith, however, as the following verses indicate.

VERSES 49–50

My eyes pour down unceasingly, without stopping, until the Lord looks down / and sees from heaven

Jeremiah weeps intensely and by example calls the remnant to let their "eyes pour down unceasingly, without stopping." But these tears are not without hope. Verse 50 uses the preposition *until*. Jeremiah would tenaciously weep for Judah and Israel "until Yahweh looks down and sees from heaven." Here, hope is born. Implicit is a beseeching of His mercy. Once again, the merciful "look" of Yahweh is the essence of hope (cf. Lamentations 1:9c, 11c, 20a; 2:20a). The prophet believed that if the people would truly repent of their sin and return to Him, God would look upon them with favor once again and restore them.

Jeremiah modeled a tenacity of faith, which was based upon the promises of the Word of God and the merciful character of the LORD. He would not stop weeping until Yahweh acted in mercy. See Psalm 102:19 (see Psalm 102:17, 19–21; cf. Deuteronomy 26:15). See also Psalm 80:15 in the context of the entire Psalm.

VERSE 51

My eyes bring pain to my soul / because of all the daughters of my city

Jeremiah's faith did not ease the temporal pain of all he saw with his eyes. He shared God's perspective on the horror and foolishness of it all (cf. Jeremiah 4:19–22). As such, Jeremiah's suffering was truly empathetic and representative. He suffered *with* the people, *for* the people, and *because of* the people. The phrase "all the daughters of my city" is plural, in contrast to the similar phrase "daughter of my people" in verse 48. Note the singular in 4:3, 10. This may be a poetic reference to the destruction of the towns and villages near Jerusalem (Numbers 21:25) or perhaps a reference to the suffering of the women in particular (cf. 5:11).

VERSE 52

My enemies without cause / hunted me down like a bird

It is possible that verses 52–54 speak of the prophet's own imprisonment in the pit, as described in Jeremiah 38:4–13, or on some other occasion not recorded in Scripture. It is perhaps possible that he was speaking as a representative of the remnant. The invading forces no doubt "hunted" the remaining inhabitants of Jerusalem after the walls were breached. Psalm 35:7 says, "For without cause they hid their net for me; without cause they dug a pit for my soul." Note the hunting imagery of 4:18–19 (cf. Psalm 11:1–2; 124:7; Jeremiah 16:16; Ezra 13:20).

If this is Jeremiah's personal testimony, as the grammar indicates, evidently faith has changed his perspective. The prophet relates to the suffering of the people by describing the personal affliction he experienced at the hands of his enemies. A number of examples of Jeremiah's suffering are recorded in his larger book: He endured death threats and attempts on his life (Jeremiah 11:19–20 and 26:7–8); he was beaten and imprisoned (Jeremiah 37:14–16 and 38:3–6). He views his difficult circumstances realistically, as verses 52–54 reveal, but it does not lead him to despair (contrast vv. 1–18).

VERSE 53

They have silenced me in the pit / and have placed a stone on me

Joseph was placed in a pit by his brothers (Genesis 37:29). Jeremiah had been placed in the pit (Jeremiah 38:6–13). Here is a man who understands affliction. He knows suffering firsthand. He knows the condition of the oppressed because he has been there. Both verse 55 and Psalm 88:3–6 indicate that the "pit" can refer to the grave—the place of the dead. Many English versions translate the word *stone* as plural—"they flung me alive into the pit and cast stones on me" (ESV). But the Hebrew word for *stone* is singular and more simply pictures the stone of a grave being cast upon the opening (cf. Daniel 6:17). They did not throw him into the pit thinking they would come back later and take him out (like one of the brothers of Joseph did in Genesis 37:22). But they threw him into a pit, placing a stone over it, in order to make it his grave.

Jeremiah was recalling the testing of faith that involved being hunted and facing death. Both he personally and the nation corporately experienced the terror of being prey for their enemies and were faced with the silence of the pit. Faith is confirmed by testing—and here Jeremiah acknowledged the severity of the test.

Verse 54

Waters flowed over my head; I said, "I am cut off!"

According to Jeremiah 38, while in the pit, Jeremiah sank into the mud and was in danger of dying. There was no mention of flowing water in that passage. Here, however, the prophet writes of "waters" flowing over his head, so much so that he declared, "I am cut off!" David's song in Psalm 69:1–4 may give insight into Jeremiah's words here:

> Save me, O God, for the waters have threatened my life. I have sunk in deep mire, and there is no foothold; I have come into deep waters, and a flood overflows me. I am weary with my crying; my throat is parched; my eyes fail while I wait for my God. Those who hate me without a cause are more than the hairs of my head; those who would destroy me are powerful, being wrongfully my enemies.

Whether Jeremiah was speaking of personal experience only or as a representative of the remnant's national experience, it is clear that his words depict the testing of faith in desperate circumstances.

Verse 55

I called on Your name, O Lord, out of the lowest pit

This sounds like Jonah, who prayed something very similar from the belly of the fish: "I called out of my distress to the Lord, and He answered me. I cried for help from the depth of Sheol; You heard my voice" (Jonah 2:2). Here Jeremiah testifies to this call of faith, as does the psalmist in Psalm 18:5–6; 116:3–4; 118:5; 120:1; 130:1–2; 138:3 (see also Romans 10:13). In light of Jeremiah's previous allusion to Psalm 69, he may have been meditating on verses 13–15 of that Psalm:

But as for me, my prayer is to You, O LORD, at an acceptable time; O God, in the greatness of Your lovingkindness, answer me with Your saving truth. Deliver me from the mire and do not let me sin; may I be delivered from my foes and from the deep waters. May the flood of water not overflow me nor the deep swallow me up, nor the pit shut its mouth on me.

The triumph of faith and the assurance of deliverance start when we look to the LORD alone for our deliverance. The name or character of Yahweh is revealed in the Scriptures. "Out of the lowest pit," the poet called upon the character of Israel's covenant-keeping God—Yahweh—and, according to the next verse, He heard.

VERSE 56

You have heard my voice, do not hide Your ear from my prayer for relief, from my cry for help

The great compassion of the LORD is evident in that Jeremiah was confident Yahweh had "heard [his] voice." As Jeremiah called out to the Lord from the pit, the Lord heard and delivered him. Psalm 31:22 also says, "As for me, I said in my alarm, 'I am cut off from before Your eyes'; nevertheless You heard the voice of my supplications when I cried to You."

VERSE 57

You drew near when I called on you; You said, "Do not fear!"

Again, echoes of Psalm 69 can be heard in Jeremiah's words here: "Oh draw near to my soul and redeem it; ransom me because of my enemies" (Psalm 69:18). The prophet here expresses confidence that God had drawn near when he called. When Jeremiah cried out to Him, God became his Redeemer. Such nearness brought comfort. Psalm 145:18: "The LORD is near to all who call upon Him, to all who call upon Him in truth."

The words *do not fear* were also used in Jeremiah 30:10; 46:27–28 in the context of national restoration. God's presence and promises bring comfort to His people.

VERSE 58

O Lord, You have pleaded my soul's cause; you have redeemed my life

God provided help by executing His justice upon the enemies of Jeremiah. The Hebrew literally reads: "You have pleaded, *Adonai*, the pleadings of my soul" or "You have contended, *Adonai*, the contentions of my soul." The Sovereign Master has taken the role of advocate and defender (cf. 1 John 2:1–2), and Jeremiah is entrusting himself to the judge of heaven. Psalm 35:1 has a related thought expressed in petition: "Contend, O LORD, with those who contend with me; fight against those who fight against me." In Jeremiah 51:36, God had promised what the prophet was now convinced of: "Therefore thus says the LORD, 'Behold, I am going to plead your case.'" While the context of Jeremiah 51 is judgment upon Babylon, this would vindicate God's promise in Genesis 12:3 and imply His faithfulness to the blessings portion of the Abrahamic covenant.

The word *redeemed, "goel"* in Hebrew, speaks of being delivered from bondage, vindicated and protected. Again, it was used in Psalm 69:18, which Jeremiah may have been meditating on as he wrote this song. See also Psalm 103:4; 106:10; 107:2 (cf. Psalm 119:154). Proverbs 23:11 couples the idea of God as Redeemer and as advocate/defender, speaking of the fatherless: "For their Redeemer is strong; He will plead their case against you."

VERSE 59

O LORD, You have seen my oppression; judge my case

The word for "oppression" is used only here in the Scriptures. It refers to a deprivation of justice[3]. The confidence of faith is that Yahweh sees injustice by means of His holy omniscience. And being just, He will indeed "judge" rightly concerning the injustices endured by His people. Here the prophet calls for that judgment to come. The cry is akin to those in heaven, who had been slain because of the Word of God, as Revelation 6:10 records: "How long, O Lord, holy and true, will You refrain from judging and avenging our blood on those who dwell on the earth?" Jesus did exactly the same when He was oppressed and tormented by His enemies. First Peter 2:23 testifies, "and while being reviled,

---

3   Francis Brown, *Enhanced Brown-Driver-Briggs Hebrew and English Lexicon* (Oxford, Clarendon Press, 1906).

He did not revile in return; while suffering, He uttered no threats, but kept entrusting Himself to Him who judges righteously" (see also Psalm 43:1).

VERSE 60

You have seen all their vengeance, all their schemes against me
Again, this could apply to the specific events that led up to Jeremiah 11:19–20 or to some other incident. Others suggest that Jeremiah was speaking as the representative of the remnant in Israel. But the point is clear: The believer trusts that *God sees* all injustice and all vengeance, and all schemes against His people. *Schemes* refers to "thoughts" and "plans" of ill.

The trust/confidence of faith rests in the truth that *the LORD sees*.

VERSE 61

You have heard their reproach, O LORD, all their schemes against me
Yahweh—Israel's covenant-keeping God—not only has seen, but He also has heard the enemy's reproach, their mocking songs and whispered threats. This continues the imagery of God's holy omniscience in the context of trust in His love and justice. The final phrase, "all their schemes against me," is repeated from verse 60. Psalm 56:5 also uses the same expression, though translated differently: "all their *thoughts* are against me."

See Psalm 56 for a song that parallels both Jeremiah's tears and confidence here.

VERSE 62

The lips of my assailants and their whispering / against me all day long
Again note the parallel in Jeremiah's personal life as described in Jeremiah 18:18–20. Psalm 59:7–8, 12–13 says:

Behold, they belch forth with their mouth; swords are in their lips, for they say, "Who hears?" But You, O LORD, laugh at them; You scoff at all the nations.... On account of the sin of their mouth and the words of their lips, let them even be caught in their pride, and on account of

curses and lies which they utter. Destroy them in wrath, destroy them
that they may be no more; that men may know that God rules in Jacob
to the ends of the earth.

The psalmist was concerned about God's reputation, holiness, and justice.
Here Jeremiah is confident that the LORD both sees and hears the injustice and
slander.

VERSE 63

Look on their sitting and their rising; I am their mocking song
The imperative *look* is a plea for God to "consider" (cf. Psalm 13:3) the ways of
the enemies of His remnant. The "mocking song" is reminiscent of 3:14, but
this time Jeremiah is calling for Yahweh's holy consideration rather than simply
recounting his own despair.

VERSE 64

You will recompense them, O LORD, according to the work of their hands
God *will* pay the prophet's enemies back for their wicked deeds. Verses 64–66
are rightly translated as future realities rather than imperatives (cf. KJV, NIV,
etc.). This is an assertion of trust and confidence. Though the prophet was
most likely referring to those within his own nation who opposed him, he
undoubtedly knew Yahweh's just character from the words of his own sermon,
as recorded in Jeremiah 51:6: "Flee from the midst of Babylon, and each of you
save his life! Do not be destroyed in her punishment, for this is the LORD's time
of vengeance; He is going to render recompense to her." Isaiah 35:3–4 says,
"Encourage the exhausted, and strengthen the feeble. Say to those with anxious
heart, 'Take courage, fear not. Behold, your God will come with vengeance; the
recompense of God will come, but He will save you.'" If Yahweh would execute
justice upon Babylon—the very nation that served as His rod of chastening
upon Israel—certainly he would "recompense" the enemies who opposed His
prophet, Jeremiah (see also Psalm 28:4–5; Jeremiah 10:25; 11:20; 2 Timothy
4:14; Revelation 6:10; 18:6–8).

Verse 65

You will give them hardness of heart, your curse will be on them

The phrase "hardness of heart" is translated as "sorrow of heart" in the KJV. It seems to speak of an obstinacy and spiritual blindness of the heart.[4] The NIV translates it: "Put a veil over their hearts." As illustrated by Pharaoh in the book of Exodus (Exodus 4:21; 7:3, 13, 22; 8:15, 19, 32; 9:7, 12, 34–35; 10:1, 20, 27; 11:10; 14:4, 8; cf. 1 Samuel 6:6), God sovereignly hardens the hearts of those who harden their own heart and refuse to submit to His authority. Deuteronomy 2:10 gives another illustration: "But Sihon king of Heshbon was not willing for us to pass through his land; for the LORD your God hardened his spirit and made his heart obstinate, in order to deliver him into your hand as he is today." In other words, Jeremiah prayed that *God* would give His enemies that which *they* actively sought—autonomy of heart against the one true and living God.

God's "curse" in this context is described by the previous statement—a "covered heart." Proverbs 3:33 says, "The curse of the LORD is on the house of the wicked, but He blesses the dwelling of the righteous" (though a different word for *curse* is used).

Verse 66

You will pursue them in anger and destroy / them from under the heavens of the LORD

Just as God pursued Judah and chastened her for her rebellion, God will chase down His enemies until they are destroyed. Jeremiah was now confident of God's covenant promises to His people. Rather than exposing a vindictive spirit bent on revenge, the prophet was clinging to the revealed Word of God. Deuteronomy 30:7 gave a promise to the remnant when they turned to Him: "The LORD your God will inflict all these curses [cf. Deuteronomy 28–29] on your enemies and on those who hate you, who persecuted you." A New Testament parallel is found in 2 Thessalonians 1:6–10.

---

4 Francis Brown, *Enhanced Brown-Driver-Briggs Hebrew and English Lexicon* (Oxford, Clarendon Press, 1906).

Jeremiah ends this chapter of hope with an affirmation that the LORD is faithful to His promises. This is the confidence of faith—the LORD sees, the LORD hears, and the LORD will be faithful to His Word.

INSIGHTS FOR COUNSELING

Even after we embrace the loyal love and tender mercies of God in the aftermath of His discipline, all of life's problems do not suddenly disappear. Suffering is ever-present, and it is always painful no matter the cause. However, no affliction is more internally tormenting than that which is the result of our own sinful choices. When that is the case, what do we do? How do we return to the sweet path of God's blessing that is characterized by inner peace in the midst of turmoil? How do we move from the paralysis of regret to the freedom of forgiveness?

The answers are laid out plainly in Lamentations 3. Tracing the chapter as a whole, we learn that we can enumerate our sorrows and grief in detail, but if left there, we only despair (vv. 1–18). We must embrace the LORD's loving-kindness—grab hold of the truth of the revelation of God about the character of God and not let go no matter the circumstances (vv. 19–39). And then we must continue to express our repentance and determined faith in prayer and supplication (vv. 40–66).

Only when hope is renewed by faith will a suffering believer have the resources to turn away from sinful self-focus and compassionately call others to repentance and confession of their sin. Here we may recall the words of King David in the wake of his own suffering: "Restore to me the joy of Your salvation and sustain me with a willing spirit. Then I will teach transgressors Your ways, and sinners will be converted to You" (Psalm 51:12–13). When reaching out to others, we who have experienced God's mercy must remain realistic about the consequences of our own sin that still exist and also be mindful of our need to maintain a tenacious faith that clings to God's promises when severely tested. This realistic mindset will mature as we intentionally think on certain biblical principles.

1. Biblical repentance is primarily an act of the will, not emotion.

It is a determined choice to place oneself under the authority of God. Lamentations 3:40 begins with a choice: "*Let us* examine and probe our ways." This is an act of the will, not emotion. Feelings may follow repentance, but they are never the primary pavers of the road toward it. Yes, there is a godly sorrow that leads to repentance. However, it is a sorrow that is informed and aggravated by truth. True repentance is based on hearing God's Word and results in obedience that is characterized by submission to His authority. Repentance confesses, "God, You are right. I am wrong. What You say in Your Word is true. I am a rebel and a liar" (Lamentations 3:40; 2 Corinthians 7:9–10).

2. When God disciplines us for our sin, there is only one acceptable response.

We must humbly examine our ways, repent, and return to the Lord. Only then will He freely pardon. This agrees with Isaiah 55:6–7, "Seek the Lord while He may be found; call upon Him while He is near. Let the wicked forsake his way and the unrighteous man his thoughts; and let him return to the Lord, and He will have compassion on him, and to our God, for He will abundantly pardon." In the book of Acts, Peter preached this same message to the Jews who had crucified Jesus: "Therefore repent and return, so that your sins may be wiped away, in order that times of refreshing may come from the presence of the Lord" (3:19).

Unfortunately, not all people respond to the Lord in this way. For example, some believers have an entitlement mentality—that is, they think that simply because they are Christians, they are entitled to a life free of pain and suffering. Then when suffering comes on the scene, they become angry at God and actually feel justified in their anger. All the while the Spirit of God is calling to them, "Won't you wake up? Won't you realize that what you are suffering is the result of your own sinful choices? Repent and you will find the compassion and hope I am waiting to give to you through the application of biblical truth to life." This call to repentance is clear. As sinners, we sometimes have the audacity to think that God must accept us on our terms. But that is not true. God is God. We are not. He is under no obligation. We must come to God on His terms, not ours. And His terms include honest repentance (Lamentations 3:40–42).

3. Sin brings painful consequences, but God brings hope.

The consequences of sin are sent by God to awaken us to the seriousness of our disobedience so that we will turn from our errors and return to the Lord in obedience to His Word. This then returns us to the place of His blessing. Hope produced by faith does not remove the distressing consequences of sin. We may weep tears of grief for a long time. We may have to live with the painful results of our sin until the day we see the Lord, but that does not mean we must live without hope. God gives us hope as we repeatedly turn to Him. This persevering faith produces a hope that endures through the midst of our pain (Lamentations 3:49–50; Romans 5:3–5).

4. We need to honestly admit our guilt by means of biblical confession.

Biblical confession leads to forgiveness and restoration. It is not the same as saying, "I'm sorry." To *confess* means to agree with God's view of our sin. When I confess my sin before God, what I am really saying is this: "Lord, Your view of my sin is accurate. I now agree with it. I will stop making excuses. I will stop blaming others. I will finally admit that this sin is *my* problem. It is *I* who have sinned against You, and therefore I need Your forgiveness." When we truly confess our sin to God in this way, "He is faithful and righteous to forgive us our sins and to cleanse us from all unrighteousness" (1 John 1:9). We need to be honest before the Lord.

Many do not experience sweetness of fellowship with the Lord because they never get beyond apologizing to Him. And too often we are so preoccupied with other people's sins that we fail to see our own, especially in the heat of an interpersonal conflict. Biblical confession, however, honestly admits to God that we are guilty and therefore deserving of the judgment His Word pronounces upon our sin. We must follow Judah's example of repentance by declaring to God, "We have transgressed and rebelled" (Lamentations 3:42).

This same principle of honesty in confession applies to our relationships with people. Many go through life unknowingly building walls in their relationships because they never move beyond mere apology to confession. "I apologize" is what we say when we trip over someone's foot. An apology admits no guilt, just a mistake. In contrast, biblical confession admits moral guilt. It says, "I was wrong. I sinned against you by…[insert specific action here]." Perhaps there are some husbands or wives who have never said to one another, "I was wrong. Will you please forgive me?" As a result, the sin that hinders their relationship is not actually dealt with in a cleansing, restorative manner. They need to learn to practice biblical confession that says, "I was wrong. I hurt you. Will you please forgive me?" as well as the habit of biblical forgiveness that says, "Yes, in light of all that God has forgiven me, I forgive you." The difference between a confession and an apology is that one openly admits sin while the other does not. We must learn to practice true confession that admits culpability, and discipline ourselves to humbly receive God's forgiveness for our own sin and then freely grant that same release of debt to others who sin against us (Ephesians 4:31–32; Colossians 3:12–13).

5. God draws near to those who cry out to Him in humble repentance.

James 4:7–8 says it this way, "Submit therefore to God. Resist the devil and he will flee from you. Draw near to God and He will draw near to you. Cleanse your hands, you sinners; and purify your hearts, you double-minded." God draws near to us when we get serious about turning from our sin. The Christian life needs to be a continual walk of repentant faith. Until we see the Lord face-to-face, there will never be a time in which we do not need to turn from sin, as the Spirit convicts us, and draw near to God. He will then draw near to us. God hears the believer's penitent, humble cry for deliverance, mercy, and compassion (Lamentations 3:55–58; Psalm 34:18; Psalm 51:1).

6. When we are oppressed and afflicted by enemies, we need to entrust ourselves to God.

We must follow the examples of Jeremiah and Jesus. As Jeremiah recounted the deeds of Judah's enemies, he rested in the omniscience of God, who knew every thought, word, and action of Judah's enemies. "You have seen all their vengeance, all their schemes against me," he prayed (Lamentations 3:61). As the author of Hebrews reminds us, "There is no creature hidden from His sight, but all things are open and laid bare to the eyes of Him with whom we have to do" (4:13). When Jesus was oppressed, condemned, and unjustly executed by the enemies of God, He entrusted Himself to God as the final Judge. So must we (Lamentations 3:59–66; Psalm 33:13; 1 Peter 2:21–23). Psalm 9:10 affirms, "Those who know Your name will put their trust in you, for You, O LORD, have not forsaken those who seek You." Entrusting ourselves to God means we must seek to know His character and ways. If we don't know the character and ways of God as revealed in His Word (His "name"), then we will have no stronghold, no one trustworthy, and we will trust in something or someone who will forsake us. But praise be to God that He never forsakes those who seek Him!

7. A tenacious faith incessantly seeks the Lord's mercy through prayer and supplication.

The testing of one's faith in desperate circumstances confirms its genuine nature and results in the triumph of assurance of deliverance. In the time of trouble, Jeremiah knew where to turn—and he kept turning there. How many a sufferer has prayed only a short time and then given up for lack of faith and habit? Prayer must be a way of life for us, an attitude. Only then will we be obedient to the command to "pray without ceasing" (1 Thessalonians 5:17). Like the unprotected widow in Jesus' parable refused to stop seeking legal protection until she received it, we must tirelessly knock on the doors of heaven by means of prayer until life-sustaining mercy is showered upon us in our time of need. God invites us to weep and to draw near to Him in our times of grief (Lamentations 3:48–51; Luke 18:1–8; Hebrews 4:14–16).

8. God's people need to have the Word of God streaming through their every thought.

Jeremiah's poem alludes to countless other passages in the Old Testament. He drew comfort, strength, and truth from the Scriptures and processed them so as to comfort and exhort others as well. If we do not cultivate godly habits of prayer and scriptural meditation, we will be much more susceptible to despair and hopelessness. If we fill our minds with God's truth, thankfulness to God and edification of others will mark our lives. Remember Colossians 3:16: "Let the word of Christ richly dwell within you, with all wisdom teaching and admonishing one another with psalms and hymns and spiritual songs, singing with thankfulness in your hearts to God." God's comfort and hope are often measured out to us through His Word. Therefore, we need to discipline ourselves to daily feast upon Scripture so that we will be governed by the mind of Christ (Luke 4:3–4; 1 Corinthians 2:12–16; 2 Corinthians 10:5).

HOMEWORK FOR COUNSELING

You are encouraged to photocopy homework pages for use in personal counseling.

Part 1: Thinking Rightly About Sin and About God

Read again Lamentations 3:40–66.

1. What specific sins do you need to repent of and confess to God?

2. What does it mean to *confess* sin to God and to others (note v. 42)? How is a confession different than an apology?

3. Write out a prayer of repentance that includes a cry to God for help and mercy.

4. From Lamentations 3:52–66, list all the ways Jeremiah's enemies oppressed him. Are you being oppressed by enemies? How are you presently responding to them? Meditate on 1 Peter 2:22–23. How does your response need to change so as to more accurately reflect Jesus?

5. Read again verses 49-50. Have you allowed yourself to weep in your time of grief? Jesus wept over the death of His friend, Lazarus (John 11:35). Though His grief was not caused by sin, this example reminds us that weeping is not sin, and that our God is a God of compassion and comfort (2 Cor. 1:3). Take time to pray, admitting your need for God's compassion, and asking Him for the grace that strengthens and repairs.

Part 2: Hoping in Jesus

Perhaps throughout this chapter you have been thinking, *Yes, I see how God dealt with Judah's sin and why He called them to repentance. But that is the harsh God of the Old Testament. The loving God of the New Testament would never treat people that way.* However, the New Testament warns of God's judgment upon hardened unbelievers.

> For after all it is only just for God to repay with affliction those who afflict you, and to give relief to you who are afflicted and to us as well when the Lord Jesus will be revealed from heaven with His mighty angels in flaming fire, dealing out retribution to those who do not know God and to those who do not obey the gospel of our Lord Jesus. (2 Thessalonians 1:6–8)

Man has a window of time to repent. However, when God decides this window will be shut, the Lord Jesus will return from heaven. The One who came the first time as Savior will come the second time as Judge. He will judge all who have not obeyed the gospel call to repent and believe. He will pursue to the end all who reject His free offer of salvation. He will then cast them into the Lake of Fire, where they will exist forever, separated from God (Revelation 20:11–15). The only way to escape this eternal punishment is by running to Jesus in repentant faith, for He bore the wrath of God in our place (see Romans 5:6–11). Because Jesus endured the wrath of God against sin, we do not have to—*if* we turn from our sinful ways and return to the Lord.

The New Testament also soberly reminds us that God disciplines believers—those He loves as His own children:

> It is for discipline that you endure; God deals with you as with sons; for what son is there whom his father does not discipline? But if you are without discipline, of which all have become partakers, then you are illegitimate children and not sons. (Hebrews 12:7–8)

As believers in Christ, we must pursue a lifestyle of repentance, responding in submissive obedience to God's chastening love. We must learn to be trained by His discipline whether we feel like it or not. Nowhere in the Word of God do we find God saying that we should *feel* repentant first. He commands us, "Repent!" When we humbly admit our disobedience to God, receive His cleansing mercy, and submit to His Word, then we move forward in our growth toward maturity in Christ.

1. Make a list of how the Lord has been faithful in your life in the past—be specific and take time to survey your entire life.
2. Write out a prayer thanking Him for these providential acts, deliverances, protections, provisions, etc.

Chapter 6

"Looking for Help Was Useless"

A Song of Sin and Degradation—
Yet Solace and Deliverance

Lamentations 4:1–22

Jeremiah 29:11 is probably the most popular high school and college graduation verse, but we need to remember that it was first given to people who were about to experience suffering beyond their imagination. "'For I know the plans that I have for you,' declares the LORD, 'plans for welfare and not for calamity to give you a future and a hope'" (Jeremiah 29:11). What does this mean? God said He did not have plans for calamity, but what Judah experienced certainly looks like calamity. After all, Jeremiah himself says of her, "For your ruin is as vast as the sea" (Lamentations 2:13).

What we discover is that God knew their hearts. He knew where they were placing their hope and trust. Therefore, He chose to strip away every earthly thing that tempted them to shift their hope away from Him. God's "future and hope" for them included incomprehensible pain that would position them more firmly on the rock of His mercy.

In chapters 1–2 of Lamentations, there is an obvious intensity and building of emotion. In chapter 3, the book crescendos with repentance and faith—taking refuge in Yahweh's lovingkindness and goodness. But Jerusalem didn't suddenly rebuild itself, loved ones didn't come back to life, and babies didn't instantly find food. The reality was that the ensuing generations would have to slowly recover from the holocaust and destruction of Zion.

Chapter 4, though still quite grim, communicates more of a settled objectivity, which helps the sufferer learn to deal less emotionally with the realities of life after tragedy. Even after we have turned to the LORD in repentance and faith—embracing His loyal love and tender mercies—the temporal consequences of sin remain (whether they are directly related to our own sin or to the sin of others). However, once we come to the realization of our guilt and embrace the great faithfulness of God, we find that we have been given all we need to live not as victims, but as victors.

In Lamentations 4 we see three sections of Jeremiah's song that more objectively chronicle the realities of continuing consequences of the siege of Jerusalem and the sins of her people. But it ends with a note of resolute confidence in God's Word, as well as a promise they could bank on: "The punishment of your iniquity has been completed, O daughter of Zion; he will exile you no longer" (v. 22).

TEACHING OUTLINES

Option A
Seeking God in the Wake of Sin's Misery
   I.   A song of sorrow and despair (1:1–22)
  II.   A song of sovereignty and divine discipline (2:1–22)
 III.   A song of suffering and determination/dependence/hope (3:1–66)
  IV.   A song of sin and degradation—yet solace and deliverance (4:1–22)
        A. Realism concerning the siege's consequences (vv. 1–12)
            1. The degradation of the people (vv. 1–7)
                a. Degraded (vv. 1–2)
                    i.   The way it was—pure gold and precious stones (vv. 1)
                    ii. The way it is—pottery/earthen jars (v. 2)
                b. Dehumanized (vv. 3–5)

        i. The illustration from the animal world (v. 3)

        ii. The infant ignored (v. 4)

        iii. The ignoble plight of the wealthy (v. 5)

     c. Divinely judged (v. 6)

  2. The degradation of the princes (vv. 7–12)

     a. Degraded (vv. 7–8)

        i. The way it was (v. 7)

        ii. The way it is (v. 8)

     b. Dehumanized (vv. 9–10)

        i. Better to have been slaughtered than starve (v. 9)

        ii. Boiled their own children for food (v. 10)

     c. Divinely judged (vv. 11–12)

        i. By the wrath of Yahweh (v. 11)

        ii. With the world in disbelief (v. 12)

B. Realism concerning sin's consequences (vv. 13–20)

  1. The sins of the prophets and priests (vv. 13–16)

     a. Their bloodshed (v. 13)

     b. Their blindness and bloody defilement (v. 14)

     c. Their banishment (vv. 15–16)

  2. The sins of the people—placing their hope in human deliverers (vv. 17–20)

     a. They looked to a nation that could not save (v. 17)

     b. They languished under the pursuit of their hunters (vv. 18–19)

     c. They lost their messiah—King Zedekiah—to the enemy (v. 20)

C. Resoluteness/confidence concerning God's promises (vv. 21–22)

  1. The promise of the cup for the daughter of Edom (v. 21)

  2. The promise of comfort for the daughter of Zion (v. 22a)

  3. The promise of chastisement for the daughter of Edom (v. 22b)

Option B

I.   The consequences (vv. 1–12)

  A. Painful humiliation (vv. 1–2)

  B. Extreme hunger (vv. 3–5; 7–10)

  C. Divine judgment (vv. 6, 11–12)

II. The causes (vv. 13–20)

    A. Disloyalty of the spiritual leaders (vv. 13–16)

    B. Dependence on man's help (vv. 17–20)

III.   The consummation (vv. 21–22)

EXPOSITION
VERSE 1

How dark the gold has become, the pure gold has changed! The sacred stones are poured out / at the corner of every street.

As in 1:1 and 2:1, Jeremiah begins this fourth poem with the word *how—alas*. But unlike the first chapters, the following poem is more objective and less emotional in tone. After the crescendo of chapter 3 and the renewed faith in the lovingkindness of the LORD, chapter 4 chronicles the remaining pain honestly, but now through the lens of God's faithfulness.

    Though some have understood verse 1 as a reference to the gold and sacred stones of the temple, it seems that those who sacked the city would have taken anything of earthly value. Moreover, gold does not technically tarnish or change. Second Chronicles 3:6 says this of the temple Solomon built: "Further, he adorned the house with precious stones; and the gold was gold from Parvaim." But again, the valuables would have already been looted. A generation later, Zechariah would write of God's people as "the stones of a crown, sparkling in His land" (Zechariah 9:16). Verse 2 indicates that the gold and sacred stones are the people of God, "the precious sons of Zion." The people are the ones worth their weight in gold. Exodus 19:5 refers to Israel as God's treasured possession.

VERSE 2

The precious sons of Zion, weighed against fine gold, how they are regarded as earthen jars, the work of a potter's hands!

The KJV captures the thought: "The precious sons of Zion, comparable to fine gold." This identifies the gold and precious stones that were tarnished and discarded respectively in verse 1. Jeremiah writes of how it once was: "The precious sons of Zion were worth their weight in gold" (NET). Once, God's people were a treasure; now "they are regarded as earthen jars, the work of a potter's hands"— common, fragile vessels of clay. The prophet had predicted this in Jeremiah 18, where God told him to visit a potter's house to watch how the master craftsman patiently dealt with the lump of clay, working it over and over in his hands to form it into his own creation. The point was that Judah is the clay in the divine Potter's hand. God is gracious and compassionate but also sovereign, and He can do with the clay whatever He chooses. Additionally, in the next chapter (Jeremiah 19), the prophet is told to purchase a clay pot in the sight of the older men and priests of Judah. He was then to take the pot to the city dump and smash it to pieces to demonstrate that God is the sovereign Potter who has the right to pour out His judgment upon Judah because she sacrificed her children to Baal. As Constable notes, "Earthenware pottery was of such little value in the ancient Near East that people would not repair it but simply replaced it."[1] And that is what came to pass. The people were warned by God, but they would not listen. Once viewed as a valuable treasure, Judah was now discarded as a common vessel, thrown onto the refuse pile.

After embracing the mercy and faithfulness of the LORD in chapter 3, Jeremiah continues to write realistically about the consequences of the siege, which continued to be painfully humiliating. God's prized people had been devalued from precious treasure to common vessels, broken and discarded. They had been degraded—from treasure to trash. However, what the nations that watched did not realize was that God, the faithful and sovereign Potter, was not finished with Judah yet. Yes, He had cast her aside as an impure vessel, but He was committed to her. He had made a covenant that He would keep.

VERSE 3

Even jackals offer the breast, they nurse their young; but the daughter of my people has become cruel / like ostriches in the wilderness

The word for *jackals* here was often used in the contexts of judgment and desolation (Job 30:29; Isaiah 34:13; 43:20; Micah 1:8, where "jackals" are paired with "ostriches"). God had previously warned them through the mouth of Jeremiah, "I will make Jerusalem a heap of ruins, a haunt of jackals; and I will make the cities of Judah a desolation, without inhabitant" (Jeremiah 9:11).

The point here is that even these desert scavengers are more maternal than the

---

1   *Constable's Expository Notes on the Bible.*

Jewish mothers were in the midst of great famine and destruction. God's people had been dehumanized. The jackals had more to feed their young than the people of God did. (It is also possible that Jeremiah has in mind the people of Judah, who had become less compassionate than even desert jackals. See 2:11; 3:48; 4:6 for "daughter of my people" referring to Judah as a whole.) The mothers, perhaps representative of all the inhabitants of Judah and Jerusalem, had become uncaring and "cruel like ostriches," which lay their eggs in the sand, toss a little dirt on top, and then abandon them. Job 39:13–16 reveals the ancient near east's perspective on the foolishness and cruelty of the ostrich: "The ostriches' wings flap joyously with the pinion and plumage of love, for she abandons her eggs to the earth and warms them in the dust, and she forgets that a foot may crush them, or that a wild beast may trample them. She treats her young cruelly, as if they were not hers; though her labor be in vain, she is unconcerned."

This illustration from the animal world reveals that the effects of the siege were dehumanizing. The compassion of those who had survived the siege was gone (see Isaiah 49:15). Even jackals were more gracious it would seem. And only the ostrich, with its apparently callous attitude toward its young, seemed to accurately depict Judah. Jeremiah transitions from illustration to the stark reality in verse 4.

VERSE 4

The tongue of the infant cleaves / to the roof of its mouth because of thirst; the little ones ask for bread, but no one breaks it for them

The "tongue" cleaving to the "roof of its mouth" speaks not only of dehydration, but of starvation to the point of death. Psalm 22:15 says, "My strength is dried up like a potsherd, and my tongue cleaves to my jaws; and You lay me in the dust of death." The "infant" speaks of one who was not yet weaned.

Nebuchadnezzar had cut off the food supply, and there was no bread for many months. The famine was so severe that starvation was common, and parents were seeing to their own needs first (see 1:11; 2:11, 12, 19; 4:5, 9–10; 5:10).

Jeremiah wrote with honesty concerning the dehumanization of his people. They were like unclean, cruel, and foolish animals. They ignored their infants and were worse than scavengers. Verse 5 continues the inglorious record. Starvation was not reserved for babies and toddlers.

VERSE 5

*Those who ate delicacies / are desolate in the streets; those reared
in purple / embrace ash pits*

They who were raised in royalty are now going to the garbage pile or dunghill
to find food. *Delicacies* is elsewhere translated "delight" (Proverbs 29:17) and
"dainties" (Genesis 49:20). As with the parallel statement that follows, this is a
reference to the wealthy (2 Samuel 1:24; Luke 16:19). Those who used to eat
delightful food are now bereft of everything and evidently living on the streets.

Jeremiah continues to realistically chronicle Israel's devaluation and dehumanization. Though he had embraced God's mercy and faithfulness (3:21–25),
the horrible temporal conditions remained. Verse 6 reveals the cause of such
degrading consequences.

VERSE 6

*For the iniquity of the daughter of my people / is greater than the
sin of Sodom, which was overthrown as in a moment, and no hands
were turned toward her.*

Iniquity speaks of both guilt and punishment for iniquity. Both the sin and
the punishment of Israel were "greater" than that of Sodom's, which was ram-
pant homosexuality, for which the city, along with its neighbor Gomorrah, was
destroyed by fire from heaven (Genesis 19). Sodom did not have the privilege
of being God's covenant nation, nor did the people of Sodom receive the full
oracles of God as revealed to Moses and the prophets. Sodom was "overthrown
as in a moment" by God's hand. The final phrase of verse 6 is somewhat obscure
to us today. It may mean that Sodom was punished "in a moment" but that
Jerusalem's suffering lasted for decades. Sodom had no ruthless human army
starve it out and then massacre, rape, and pillage—"hands…turned against her."
Or it could mean that there was no wringing of hands in worry over a siege since
its destruction came suddenly.

Just as Sodom was divinely judged, so was Jerusalem. But Jerusalem's punishment exceeded Sodom's because her culpability before God was greater. The
people of Jerusalem had blessings the other nations never had. They possessed
God's revelation, His law. Yet they turned away from Him.

VERSE 7

Her consecrated ones were purer than snow, they were whiter
than milk; they were more ruddy in body than corals, their polishing
was like lapis lazuli

The context in verse 8 indicates that Jeremiah is no longer referring to Sodom. Rather he is once again describing Jerusalem—in this case, the "consecrated ones" of Jerusalem. The ESV reads: "Her princes were purer than snow." The KJV reads: "Her Nazarites were purer than snow." This could be a reference to all who were set apart in Israel—princes, priests, and Levites. The same root term was used of Joseph, who was distinguished above his brothers in Genesis 49:26 (see also Deuteronomy 33:16). It seems likely that Jeremiah is now referring to the leadership and its subsequent degradation during the siege and fall of Jerusalem.

The reference to "snow" and "milk" may poetically describe the fairer complexions of those raised without constant exposure to the skin-darkening rays of the sun, which would have been common among the greater populace.

Coral is translated "rubies" in the KJV. The word *polishing* means "cuttings" or "separation." It may be that they had a ruddy or reddish tint to their fair skin and sapphire/lapis lazuli (dark blue) beards.[2]

Whatever the exact reference, it is clear that Jeremiah is remembering the way it was for these separated ones before the siege and fall of Jerusalem. These leaders were once considered beautiful and valuable men, the best and brightest of the nation.

VERSE 8

There appearance is blacker than soot, they are not recognized in
the streets; their skin is shriveled on their bones, it is withered,
it has become like wood.

The "consecrated ones" are no longer beautiful. Instead, they are starving, disheveled, and dirty, covered with the soot of a burned-out city.[3] Tragedy

---

2   Walter C. Kaiser, *Grief and Pain in the Plan of God* (Fearn: Christian Focus, 2004), 108.
3   John L. Mackay, *Lamentations: A Mentor Commentary* (Fearn: Christian Focus, 2008), 187.

and destruction is no respecter of persons. It could be that their dark appearance was related to their poor health, as skin begins to darken during the process of dying. In Job 30:30, Job said, "My skin turns black on me, and my bones burn with fever." They were no longer "recognized in the streets" (2:12). The nobles were so emaciated that others don't even recognize them. They had become much like Job, who said, "My bone clings to my skin and my flesh...." (19:20). Skin that was once soft was now "dried up and withered"; it was "like wood."

The princes were now degraded like the rest of society in Jerusalem and Judah. Everyone was suffering the horrifying consequences of famine and holocaust.

VERSE 9

Better are those slain with the sword / than those slain with hunger;
for they pine away, being stricken / for lack of the fruits of the field

The ESV catches the irony of this statement: "Happier were the victims of the sword than the victims of hunger." No doubt those who were killed by sword did not view themselves as "happy," but in light of the widespread starvation, they were certainly better off. The picture here is of famine—"lack of the fruits of the field"—wounding its victims like a sword, life flowing out of them unto death. But it is a slow, torturous death.

VERSE 10

The hands of compassionate women / boiled their own children;
they became food for them / because of the destruction of the
daughter of my people

The hunger was so extreme and the desperation so great that human beings basically turned into animals. Mothers boiled their own infants and ate them. Hands that were once compassionate became cruel. Again, despite the horror of the scene, it should be noted that Jeremiah's tone here is much more matter-of-fact than his previous reference to this atrocity in 2:20a: "See, O LORD, and look! With whom have You dealt thus? Should women eat their offspring, the little ones who were born healthy?"

Boiled means to cook in a pot. The reference to "compassionate women" alludes to two passages in particular. In Deuteronomy 28:53, 56–57, written nearly 850 years before the Babylonian captivity, Moses wrote:

> Then you shall eat the offspring of your own body, the flesh of your sons and of your daughters whom the LORD your God has given you.... The refined and delicate woman among you, who would not venture to set the sole of her foot on the ground for delicateness and refinement, shall be hostile toward the husband she cherishes and toward her son and daughter, and toward her afterbirth which issues from between her legs and toward her children whom she bears; for she will eat them secretly for lack of anything else, during the siege and the distress by which your enemy will oppress you in your towns.

Yet the student of the Scriptures would have hope as he heard Jeremiah's lament. In Isaiah 49:15, it says, "Can a woman forget her nursing child and have no compassion on the son of her womb? Even these may forget, but I will not forget you." The horror may have been overwhelming, but Yahweh promised that He would not forget His people, even as He showed Himself faithful to carry out the covenant curses (see Leviticus 26:29; Deuteronomy 28:52–57; Jeremiah 19:9 [cf. Ezra 5:10; see also 2 Kings 6:26–29]). Jeremiah doesn't repeat the sickening reality in verse 10 more objectively because he wants us to become desensitized to the horror—but rather, he wanted to remind God's people that even after they have embraced God's faithful love and mercy, they must still be realistic concerning the tragic consequences of the siege, which the next verses describe as the consequences of sin.

VERSE 11

The LORD has accomplished His wrath, He has poured out His fierce anger; and He has kindled a fire in Zion / which has consumed its foundations.

Jeremiah refused to let his people think that their tragedy was merely a bad hand of cards dealt by fate. For this reason, he emphatically affirmed that it was Yahweh who had "spent His [righteous] fury" on disobedient Israel. "He [had] poured out His burning anger."

The Babylonians lit the city on fire literally, but the LORD also had "kindled a fire in Zion, which ha[d] consumed its foundations." Note Moses' song in Deuteronomy 32:22, which predicted Israel's idolatry and the LORD's wrath: "For a fire is kindled in My anger, and burns to the lowest part of Sheol, and consumes the earth with its yield, and sets on fire the foundations of the mountains." God used the literal fire to kindle a purifying fire that would change Judah's spiritual condition forever.

VERSE 12

The kings of the earth did not believe, nor did any of the inhabitants of the world, that the adversary and the enemy / could enter the gates of Jerusalem

Because of God's continual protection of Jerusalem, most notably illustrated in King Hezekiah's day (2 Kings 19:32–36), world opinion held that Israel's enemies would never be able to "enter the gates of Jerusalem" by force. But God had promised both the destruction and the surprise of the nations in Deuteronomy 29:24–28; 1 Kings 9:8–9; cf. Psalm 48:4–8; 79:1.

VERSE 13

Because of the sins of her prophets / and the iniquities of her priests, who have shed in her midst / the blood of the righteous

The prophets and priests in Israel led the people astray by both their words and example. They were unfaithful to God and disloyal to His people. This was also referenced in 2:14. The prophet wrote in Jeremiah 5:31: "The prophets prophesy falsely, and the priests rule on their own authority; and My people love it so! But what will you do at the end of it?" (see also Jeremiah 6:13–15; 8:8–12; 14:14–16; 23:11–21, 25–40 [cf. Ezra 22:26–28; Micah 3:11–12]). It is very probable that some of the religious leaders in Israel had "the righteous" put to death (as advisers of King Jehoiakim, who had the prophet Uriah executed; cf. Jeremiah 26:20–23)—something they almost did to Jeremiah himself (Jeremiah 26:8–24). But because of their false prophecies, destruction had come to Jerusalem. As Kaiser writes: "Jeremiah had warned those bleeding hearts time and time again to speak the truth, but they persisted in their 'shalom' prophecies.... The blood of all the righteous who had been slain in

Jerusalem now stained their hands. Such religious charlatans were nothing less than murderers."[4]

VERSE 14

They wandered, blind, in the streets; they were defiled with blood / so that no one could touch their garments.

The leaders in Jesus' day were just like those who opposed Jeremiah. They had a form of godliness but lacked the power of true faith. They had religion without God. They were "blind" and "defiled" (v. 14). They were of no positive spiritual benefit to the people—the blind leading the blind—because they were not lovers of truth. Instead, they hated the truth, along with those who preached it. The spiritual leaders in Judah were total failures. They did not know God. They did not love Him. Thus, they led God's people astray. The covenant curses of Deuteronomy 28:28–29 evidently came upon some of the false prophets and faithless priests: "The LORD will smite you with madness and with blindness and with bewilderment of heart; and you will grope at noon, as the blind man gropes in darkness.…" It may be that this speaks of spiritual blindness and the fact that after the horrible destruction, these false teachers had no more visions of peace—but rather, "they wandered, blind, in the streets" (cf. Micah 3:5–7). The blood of those they led astray now defiled them. "No one" came to them for spiritual guidance and prophecy. People now realized that they were unclean and defiled before the LORD.

VERSE 15

"Depart! Unclean!" they cried of themselves. "Depart, depart,
do not touch!" So they fled and wandered; men among the
nations said, "They shall not continue to dwell with us."

The translation of the phrase "they cried of themselves" is misleading. It is better to understand this as the remnant's response to those defiled religious leaders who had led them astray. The NLT renders it: "'Get away!' the people shouted at them. 'You're defiled! Don't touch us!'"

The cry "Depart! Unclean!… Depart, depart, do not touch" is reminiscent

---

4 Kaiser, 109.

of the cry of the leper in Leviticus 13:45–45. Those once beloved for the "Bible messages" of "peace" and "prosperity" were now shunned like lepers.

These false teachers led the life of vagabonds. Even "men among the nations," the Gentiles, said, "They shall not continue to dwell with us." There may be an allusion here to the banishment of Cain, who became a vagabond and wanderer on the earth because of his false Yahweh worship and the blood of the righteous he shed (cf. Genesis 4:10–14). Deuteronomy 28:65–66 reveals this as part of the covenant curses in general: "Among those nations you shall find no rest, and there will be no resting place for the sole of your foot, but there the LORD will give you a trembling heart, failing of eyes, and despair of soul. So your life shall hang in doubt before you; and you will be in dread night and day, and shall have no assurance of your life." These supposed prophets and priests were now experiencing the curse of Yahweh.

VERSE 16

The presence of the LORD has scattered them, He will not continue to regard them; they did not honor the priests, they did not favor the elders

Jeremiah literally wrote, "The face of Yahweh divided them, He will no more be looking at them." This seems to be a reference to the response of the "nations" (v. 15)—they did not "lift the face of the priests, and the old ones/elders they did not favor." It may be that the "prophets" were considered "elders" in Israel. Because God banished them, they found no honor or favor among the nations.

VERSE 17

Yet our eyes failed, looking for help was useless; in our watching we have watched / for a nation that could not save

Here we see Judah's unfaithfulness by their placing of faith in man. They were looking for help, but in all the wrong places. Notably, the prophet begins here to use the first person plural pronoun in verses 17–20. He was either including himself—perhaps identifying with the misplaced trust of the people—or poetically taking up the voice of the people.

Israel looked to Egypt for help against the Babylonians, but in the end, no help came. For in Isaiah 31:1 God warns, "Woe to those who go down to Egypt for help and rely on horses, and trust in chariots because they are many and in horsemen because they are very strong, but they do not look to the Holy One of Israel, nor seek the LORD!" (see Jeremiah 2:18, 36; 37:7–10; Ezekiel 29:6–7, 16 [cf. Isaiah 30:1–7]). Written in the first person, Lamentations 1:19a testifies of Israel: "I called to my lovers, but they deceived me."

Israel had been looking to a "nation" that could not save—instead of to Yahweh, the only real Savior and hope. They intently watched until their "eyes failed" but found out it was "useless," "vanity."

VERSE 18

They hunted our steps / so that we could not walk in our streets;
our end drew near, our days were finished / for our end had come

Because of misplaced faith and disobedience, the Jews were hunted in their own streets. Jeremiah 16:16 had warned of this: "'Behold, I am going to send for many fishermen,' declares the LORD, 'and they will fish for them; and afterwards I will send for many hunters, and they will hunt them from every mountain and every hill and from the clefts of the rocks'" (see also Lamentations 3:52). When the enemy finally broke through the wall and took over the city, they knew the "end" had come. This may well be an allusion to Amos 8:2: "He said, 'What do you see, Amos?' And I said, 'A basket of summer fruit.' Then the LORD said to me, 'The end has come for My people Israel. I will spare them no longer.'" As well, Ezekiel 7:2–7 records a prophecy that emphasized the "end."

VERSE 19

Our pursuers were swifter / than the eagles of the sky; they chased us
on the mountains, they waited in ambush for us in the wilderness.

This is likely a reference to the promise in Deuteronomy 28:49: "The LORD will bring a nation against you from afar, from the end of the earth, as the eagle swoops down, a nation whose language you shall not understand." Habakkuk 1:8 said this of the Chaldeans, "Their horses are swifter than leopards and keener than wolves in the evening. Their horsemen come galloping, their horsemen come from afar; they fly like an eagle swooping down to devour." Jeremiah wrote this concerning the enemy of the north in Jeremiah 4:13: "Behold, he goes up like clouds, and his chariots like the whirlwind; his horses are swifter than eagles. Woe to us, for we are ruined!" In light of the following verse, this may be a reference to the Babylonian capture of King Zedekiah and the scattering of his army (cf. Ezekiel 12:12–13). It may however be a general note that wherever the population fled, the enemy pursued.

Verse 20

The breath of our nostrils, the LORD's anointed, was captured
in their pits, of whom we had said, "Under his shadow / we shall
live among the nations."

"The LORD's anointed" is literally "Yahweh's messiah." This anointed one is also characterized as "the breath of our nostrils," betraying the false confidence the people had put in their king (prophets, priests, and kings were all "anointed" ones in Israel). See Jeremiah 39:5–6; 52:8–10 for the capture of Zedekiah. Israel had put her faith in a man—even their king, about whom they said, "Under his shadow we shall live among the nations." But as Psalm 91:1–2 says: "He who dwells in the shelter of the Most High will abide in the shadow of the Almighty. I will say to the LORD, 'My refuge and my fortress, My God, in whom I trust!'" (see also Jeremiah 17:5–8). King Zedekiah, who was captured and had his eyes put out, was no help to them in the hour of their need. It was as if God was saying to them, "You have gone to Egypt for help. You have trusted Zedekiah to rescue you. So this is what I will do. I will strip away every one of your earthly trusts. Egypt will not be there for you. Zedekiah will be blinded and killed." And so, by degrees, Yahweh is forcing Judah to trust in Him alone.

Verse 21

Rejoice and be glad, O daughter of Edom, who dwells in the land of Uz;
but the cup will come around to you as well, you will become drunk
and make yourself naked.

Edom was the nation to the south of Israel. The land of Uz is either an ancient synonym for Edom or the area south of Edom possessed by the Edomites (cf. Job 1; Jeremiah 25:20). The Edomites were descendants of Esau (Jacob/Israel's brother). They were related to the Jews but often played the role of bitter enemies. This was the case at the time of the destruction of Jerusalem by the Babylonians. Psalm 137:7 references the reaction of Edom to the Babylonian siege against Jerusalem: "Remember, O LORD, against the sons of Edom, the day of Jerusalem, who said, 'Raze it, raze it to its very foundation'" (see also Ezekiel 25:12–14; 35:15; 36:5; Joel 3:19). At times, it seems that Edom represented all of the enemies of God and His people (Isaiah 34:2, 6; 63:1–3).

Here, in holy sarcasm, the prophet poetically calls on the "daughter of Edom" to "rejoice and be glad." Jeremiah knew that God had promised to punish Edom (see Jeremiah 49:7–22; cf. Isaiah 34:5–6; Amos 1:11–12). God's cup of wrath will soon be poured out on them as well (see specifically Jeremiah 25:15–28; 49:7–22 [cf. Deuteronomy 30:7]). Jeremiah wrote with confidence of the LORD's promised wrath—wrath that would expose the shame of His enemies. If God's enemies insisted on rejoicing and being glad at His people's expense, then Jeremiah called them to rejoice and be glad—now would be their only reward. They too would soon be stupefied by the horrible wrath to come.

VERSE 22

The punishment of your iniquity has been completed, O daughter of Zion;
He will exile you no longer / but He will punish your iniquity, O daughter
of Edom; He will expose your sins!

God has made a commitment to His people, a commitment He will keep. Even though Judah forsook God, He faithfully chastened her in order to bring her back to Himself. He would faithfully preserve a remnant, but He would not do that for Edom. These words of hope are reminiscent of Isaiah 40:1–2: "'Comfort, O comfort My people,' says your God. 'Speak kindly to Jerusalem; and call out to her, that her warfare has ended, that her iniquity has been removed, that she has received of the LORD's hand double for all her sins'" (see also Jeremiah 46:27–28; 50:20).

The term *exile* here is related to the word translated "expose" in the second half of the verse. It would seem that Jeremiah is alluding to the future restoration of Israel and God's punishment of her enemies (Deuteronomy 30:3–7). God's discipline will eventually produce the peaceful fruit of righteousness (Hebrews 12:11). Jerusalem's nakedness will one day be covered as the LORD gathers her back from exile, but Edom's—God's enemies—will be uncovered. In Jeremiah 29:14, God declared: "'I will be found by you,' declares the LORD, 'and I will restore your fortunes and will gather you from all the nations and from all the places where I have driven you,' declares the LORD, 'and I will bring you back to the place from where I sent you into exile'" (cf. Jeremiah 30:3). In Jeremiah 32:40–42 the prophet wrote these comforting words:

> "I will make an everlasting covenant with them that I will not turn away from them, to do them good; and I will put the fear of Me in their hearts so that they will not turn away from Me. I will rejoice over them to do them good and will faithfully plant them in this land with all My heart and with all My soul." For thus says the LORD, "Just as I brought all this great disaster on this people, so I am going to bring on them all the good that I am promising them."

Jeremiah resolutely—in faith—sang of *the promised cup* Israel's enemies would drink even as he sang of *the promised comfort* for God's people. The word *punish* is literally "visit." Yahweh would surely "visit" Edom in His faithfulness and return to them the justice due their "sins." Israel's punishment would end, and they would return from exile. Edom's punishment would come, and their sin would be returned on their own heads.

As in verse 21, Jeremiah is certain that justice will be served. Thus he leaves vengeance in the hands of the LORD. He is confident in God's promises—of both salvation *and* justice. This last verse of chapter 4 of Lamentations would bring comfort for God's remnant suffering at the hands of wicked men. But it would also serve as a merciful warning to God's enemies of the certainty of judgment coming upon all who will not listen to God's Word.

INSIGHTS FOR COUNSELING

Chapter 4 presents a slight change in the book's spirit. It is less emotional than the previous three laments. Jeremiah's tears seem to have settled down a bit, and he now has a more objective view of the destruction of the city and the subsequent suffering of his people. Having come to the realization, once again, that the destruction of Jerusalem was the result of their own rebellion against God,

the people now take another significant step in their response to His chastening hand. Here they begin to name the sin and pain that has been their daily
experience. We might say that they now take full ownership of their affliction.
With the strength of the Lord, which was discovered in the third chapter, they
humbly accept the painful consequences of their sin and move forward, looking
through the lens of God's faithfulness.

Here we may learn how to more objectively process the painful reality of
sin's consequences, which remains even after repentance and the love of the
Lord has been embraced. We need to adopt a realistic view of what has happened. We aren't to ignore it or put on a fake smile and pretend everything is
wonderful. Rather, only after we properly apprehend God's mercy are we able to
humbly and honestly see the truth—and express that truth to others. There will
also be a growing confidence in God's promises—of forgiveness, restoration,
and blessing as well as the future judgment of those who reject God's grace and
mock His fallen people. Embracing the following biblical principles by faith will
empower us to work through our suffering in a manner of humble confidence
and peace.

1. God's people are precious in His sight, and He never wastes our pain.

To the onlooker, the "precious sons of Zion" appeared to be of little value,
treated like earthenware. However, nothing could be further from the truth.
God's love for His chosen people caused Him to form an irrevocable covenant
with them (Genesis 15). Therefore, this chastening was not a mark of hatred on
God's part, or a lack of value on theirs, but rather proof of His covenant love.
God is the sovereign Potter who was patiently working out the lumps in His
clay so that Israel would become a more accurate reflection of His glory. He
does the same with believers today. Therefore, we must learn to rejoice and be
thankful for the trials God sovereignly places into our lives as part of the shaping
influences that move us toward the character of Christ. God never wastes the
pain of sin. Our eyes may fail to see the spiritual profit produced by suffering,
but God's eyes never fail. His eyes are always on the goal: conforming us to the
image of His beloved Son. No matter what tribulation comes into our lives, we
are secure in the love of God in Jesus Christ our Lord (Lamentations 4:1–2;
Romans 8:28–39; James 1:2–4).

2. God is never light on sin.

Modern church culture often gives the impression that God's love trumps His justice, resulting in Him winking at our sin. But Scripture says otherwise: "God is a righteous judge, and a God who has indignation every day" (Psalm 7:11). Perhaps even more sobering is that God's Word makes it clear that He will judge His own people before He judges the wicked: "For it is time for judgment to begin with the household of God; and if it begins with us first, what will be the outcome for those who do not obey the gospel of God?" (1 Peter 4:17). The greatest proof that God's love does not eliminate His justice is the Cross of Jesus. There, He demonstrated His immense love for sinners while simultaneously judging our sin (Romans 3:21–26; 5:6–10). At the cross, the principle of Psalm 85:10 was displayed: "Lovingkindness and truth have met together; righteousness and peace have kissed each other" (Lamentations 4:6, 11).

3. Restoration to God does not necessarily remove the destruction that results from years lived as His enemy.

For example, the man who has spent most of his adult life in voluntary bondage to alcohol does not receive a new liver when he is converted to Christ. The homosexual who is redeemed by the blood of Jesus, now on his way to heaven, may still die of AIDS. Parents who lived for themselves and the world while their children were young may be forced to live the rest of their earthly lives with the painful truth that their adult son or daughter is an unbeliever. The thief who finds Jesus in a prison cell Bible study must remain in confinement until his sentence has been served. Such is the reality of life. Such is the reality of sin and the curse of its penalty. It is imperative for us to understand that experiencing God's forgiveness does not mean things will return to the way they used to be. In fact, they probably will not. Sin changes things; sin changes people; sin changes us. And we must willingly bear those enduring consequences as long as God wills (Lamentations 4:1–6).

4. We must accept God's sovereignty over the horrors of His judgment upon sin.

Too many who call themselves Christians deny God's part in tragedy. They have no problem accepting that God has a hand in the wonderful things that come into their lives, but when it comes down to accepting the fact that God is sovereign over the most horrific things they experience, they simply cannot handle it. Like Jeremiah, we must come to the place where we are able to say, "The LORD has accomplished His wrath." We may weep heartily in our suffering, but we cannot in our weeping reject the God who is sovereign over all because He is our only source of hope. Every tragedy that comes into our lives is the result of sin in a generic sense, because there was no tragedy before sin entered the world. But not all tragedy is the result of personal sin. Sometimes it is. When this is the case, we must be humble enough to admit our sin to God, accept the consequences, and move forward by His mercy and grace (Psalm 51). While in the midst of affliction, even affliction caused by our own sin, God will never forsake us. In Isaiah 49:15 [God says to Israel]: "Can a woman forget her nursing child and have no compassion on the son of her womb? Even these may forget, but I will not forget you." While this wonderful promise is given to Israel, the principle remains true for us. God says, in effect, "I will not forget you. I will not abandon you. I will walk through this dark valley with you. Just hold My hand" (Lamentations 4:9-11).

5. When God judges spiritual leaders who lead falsely, those who are led astray usually suffer with them.

Just as the "sins of her prophets" were partially responsible for the destruction of Jerusalem in the days of Jeremiah, so it is today. God holds spiritual teachers to a higher standard because of their power to influence followers, and He will one day bring all to account (James 3:1; 2 Timothy 4:1). Concerning the Pharisees, Jesus warned His disciples: "Let them alone; they are blind guides of the blind. And if a blind man guides a blind man, both will fall into a pit" (Matthew 15:14). When spiritual leaders misuse their influence, intentionally or not, the waves of God's judgment upon them often tumble upon others. For that reason, it is the responsibility of each person to discern the teachings of men by comparing them to the pure truth of the Word of God. When error is detected, it must then be rejected and God's corrective truth embraced and followed (Lamentations 4:13-16; Acts 17:11; John 4:1–3).

6. *God chastens His own people with the kind of fire that both destroys our unseen idols and purifies our faith.*

In His love for us and His jealousy for His own glory, God destroys every earthly thing we may be tempted to trust. He will tirelessly work against each false "savior" we depend on, slowly revealing to us its insufficiency. How often do we look to others—government, friends, insurance companies, doctors, etc.— and neglect the true and living God, only to find out it is an exercise in futility? When we humbly accept the consequences of sin in our lives—when we finally see what we have done—the temptation is to run to man for help. But that is not the answer. The answer is to return to the Lord. He is our only confidence.

The same fire that destroys our idols also purifies our hearts and our lives. One of the basic truths of Scripture that we must never forget is that God chastens His own. He punishes and forever casts away those who are not His own, but He disciplines His own in order to teach lessons that will change us forever. When we finally see the consequences of our sin, we may wish for a quick fire from heaven to fall down and consume us in our pain, but God has a better plan—a plan to use a slow-burning fire to purge sin from our lives so that we will come forth as gold (Lamentations 4:17; Job 23:10; 1 Peter 1:6–7).

7. *God's judgment of our enemies is always righteous and is in His perfect timing.*

When being pursued by enemies, we tend to forget God's justice and, consequently, take matters into our own hands. But we must obey Romans 12:19–21:

> Never take your own revenge, beloved, but leave room for the wrath of God, for it is written, "Vengeance is Mine, I will repay," says the Lord. "But if your enemy is hungry, feed him, and if he is thirsty, give him a drink; for in so doing you will heap burning coals on his head." Do not be overcome by evil, but overcome evil with good.

God's judgment upon unbelievers will be final, the nakedness of their sins will be exposed, and they will be forever cast away from His presence (Revelation

20:12–15). This will be a final judgment with consequences that will last for eternity. The truth of God's judgment gave David confidence as he fled from the murderous pursuits of King Saul. Remembering this same truth when we are oppressed will energize our faith and trust in God (Lamentations 4:18-22; Psalm 57:1–11).

HOMEWORK FOR COUNSELING

You are encouraged to photocopy homework pages for use in personal counseling.

PART 1: THINKING RIGHTLY ABOUT SIN AND ABOUT GOD

1. Have you named your sin yet? Be specific in listing your transgressions against God. Then spend time in prayer of confession. When you have confessed these sins to God, tear up your list or place it in a paper shredder while reciting Psalm 103:12: "As far as the east is from the west, so far has He removed [my] transgressions from [me]."

2. List ways you have been thinking of yourself as a victim rather than a victor. Confess your self-pity to God as sin. Meditate on 1 Corinthians 15:56–58.

3. Name any persons who may have tried to warn you of the dangers of choosing to walk down sinful paths. Now that your eyes have been opened to the results of your sins, do you need to go back to them and thank them for their faithful love and friendship? "Faithful are the wounds of a friend, but deceitful are the kisses of an enemy" (Proverbs 27:6).

4. Are you experiencing poor health that could be part of the consequences of God's discipline of your sin? Read James 5:13–18. Do you need to call your church elders and ask them to pray with you? Will you confess your sins to them?

5. List any false hopes or "saviors" you have been placing your trust in. Renounce these as idols, and ask God for help to turn away from them.

6. Do you have any enemies? Spend time in prayer for them, in the spirit of Jesus' command to "love your enemies and pray for those who persecute you" (Matthew 5:44). Read and pray through Psalm 57.

Part 2: Hoping in Jesus

We don't know the depth of your pain. We don't know the depth of the suffering that God has brought, or is bringing, into your life. But we do know this. Running from the One who sovereignly ordained your suffering is not the answer. There is no hope there. It is only in running *to* the One who has ordained and allowed these things to happen that you will receive hope and mercy. Don't be angry at God and thereby flee from your only source of hope and help. Humble yourself before the LORD, and run back to Him. He is the only one who can help you. And He is the only one who can clothe you with perfect righteousness to cover the nakedness of your shame (2 Corinthians 5:21). This is the gift of salvation that is found only in Jesus.

1. Read Psalm 51:17. What will God not despise?
2. Read John 1:14. How is Jesus described?
3. Read the apostle Paul's testimony found in 1 Timothy 1:12–16. How did he experience God's mercy?

In your brokenness, have you called upon the Lord for mercy?

Chapter 7

"Restore Us to You, O Lord"

A Song of Supplication and Desire for Continued Mercy and Restoration

Lamentations 5:1–22

I f you and I had written Lamentations, we would have stopped after chapter 3. We would have somehow made the pain and suffering disappear after we prayed in faith concerning God's sovereign mercy and loyal love. But God's Spirit knew it was vital to end with this fifth and final prayer—a prayer of repentant faith—a prayer that faces the reality of sin and the pain it causes while at the same time clinging to the mercy of God with a death grip. There, and there alone, hope is renewed. As Walter Kaiser notes, "The absence of the usual prayer (see Lamentations 1:20–22; 2:20–22; 3:58–66) at the end of Lamentations 4 is now supplied by the fifth chapter as a whole. It is this final touch that gives unity and completes the book, for when all is said and done we rest our case for relief and healing from suffering when we commit it to God in prayer."[1]

---

1 Walter C. Kaiser, *Grief & Pain in the Plan of God* (Fearn: Christian Focus, 2004), 113.

In many ways, Lamentations 5 seems to rehash many of the horrifying consequences of sin the people were experiencing. This tells us that sometimes pain and suffering continue long after one embraces the goodness and love of God. Though the previous chapters utilized alphabetic acrostics, chapter 5 does not. It is a less structured prayer, though it does have the same number of verses— 22—for a measure of continuity. Chapter 3 is the obvious pinnacle of the book, yet chapter 5's difference in style is also a focal point. In fact, the structure of the Hebrew poetry indicates that "things are winding down in a *decrescendo*" as Jeremiah employs "the hollow and limping metre of the *qinah* or lament poetry."[2] God's rod of discipline had brought the people of Judah to a place of brokenness and humble dependence as "the tone of the book seems to drop to a whisper."[3]

Chapter 5 helps us see that we need to keep seeking God's mercy when we feel that He has forgotten or forsaken us. Through times of great suffering, we must cry out to Him and hold to His promises, even if it is with beleaguered faith. In Lamentations 5:1–22, we see three movements that reveal the prayer for divine mercy and restoration for those who are suffering from the severe and painful consequences of sin.

TEACHING OUTLINES

Option A

Seeking God in the Wake of Sin's Misery

   I.   A song of sorrow and despair (1:1–22)

  II.   A song of sovereignty and divine discipline (2:1–22)

 III.   A song of suffering and determination/dependence/hope (3:1–66)

 IV.   A song of sin and degradation—yet solace and deliverance (4:1–22)

  V.   A song of supplication and desire [for continued mercy and restoration] (5:1–22)

       A. The continued prayer for Yahweh's merciful "look" (vv. 1–10)

           1. The supplication for mercy (v. 1)

               a. Remember what has befallen us (v. 1a)

               b. Regard our reproach (v. 1b)

---

2 Kaiser, 113.

3 Homer Heater Jr., "Structure and Meaning in Lamentations" in *Bibliotheca Sacra*, 149 (July 1992), 312.

    2. The sad situation/reproach they faced (vv. 2–10)
      a. The reproach of loss (vv. 2–5)
        i. Loss of property (v. 2)
        ii. Loss of protection (v. 3)
        iii. Loss of provisions (v. 4)
        iv. Loss of peace (v. 5)
      b. The reason for the loss (vv. 6–7)
        i. The sin of faithlessness (v. 6)
        ii. The sins of the fathers (v. 7)
      c. The reproach list continued (vv. 8–10)
        i. Helplessness in the face of oppression (v. 8)
        ii. Harm by way of bandits (v. 9)
        iii. Hunger (v. 10)
B. The consequences of sin and confession of sin (vv. 11–18)
    1. The suffering of all strata of society (vv. 11–13)
      a. The women and virgins (v. 11)
      b. The princes and elders (v. 12)
      c. The young men and youths (v. 13)
    2. The sorrow over sin's consequences (vv. 14–18)
      a. What is lost because of sin (vv. 14–16a)
        i. The gate is empty (v. 14a)
        ii. The gaiety is ceased (vv. 14b–15)
        iii. The glory is gone (v. 16a)
      b. What is gained because of sin (vv. 16b–18)
        i. Fear of judgment and faintness of heart (vv. 16b–17a)
        ii. Sorrow and a soiled testimony (vv. 17b–18)
C. The confirmation of Yahweh's sovereignty and plea for restoration (vv. 19–22)
    1. The confirmation of sovereignty—the ground of hope (v. 19)
    2. The questions in light of God's sovereignty (v. 20)
    3. The call for restoration (vv. 21–22)
      a. Restore and renew us (v. 21)
      b. Remember your covenant with us (v. 22)

Option B

   I.   "Lord, remember our reproach" (vv. 1–10)
        A. Poverty (vv. 2–4)
        B. Anxiety (v. 5)
        C. Bondage (v. 8)
        D. Theft (v. 9)
        E. Hunger (v. 10)
  II.   "Lord, we recognize the cause of our affliction" (vv. 6–7)
        A. Disloyalty (v. 6)
        B. Disobedience (v. 7)
 III.   "Lord, we realize the consequences of our rebellion" (vv. 11–18)
        A. Sexual assault (v. 11)
        B. Scandalous disregard for authority (v. 12)
        C. Slavery of the youth (v. 13)
        D. Sorrow in place of joy (vv. 14–15)
        E. Shame before other nations (v. 16)
        F. Sickness of heart (vv. 17–18)
  IV.   "Lord, restore us to Yourself" (vv. 19–22)

EXPOSITION
VERSE 1

Remember, O LORD, *what has befallen us; look, and see our reproach!*

Lamentations 5 begins with three imperatives that call for God's intervention: *remember, look,* and *see.* The first, *remember,* is more than a petition for recollection; it is a call for Yahweh's faithful mercies to be compassionately administered to His covenant people. Psalm 25:67 says: "Remember, O LORD, Your compassion and Your lovingkindnesses, for they have been from of old. Do not remember the sins of my youth or my transgressions; according to Your lovingkindness remember me, for Your goodness' sake, O LORD." The poet's earlier use of the word *remember* was a critical turning point in chapter 3 (v. 19) (see also Psalm 74:2ff; 106:4, 45–46; Jeremiah 31:20).

The phrase "what has befallen us?" or "what has happened?" is a reference to the holocaust and tragedy that now defined Judah, Jerusalem, and the Jewish people. The entire book of Lamentations is dedicated to memorializing the devastation. Verses 2–10 will once again summarize the sad situation and reproach they faced—but in a quieter, less impassioned way than the previous chapters.

Again, Yahweh's merciful look is the only real hope for the sufferer (cf. 1:9, 11, 20; 2:20; 3:50, 63). After sin and its tragic consequences have been remembered and processed from A to Z—and hope and faith have been affirmed—there is often still the need to persistently go back and petition the Lord for His mercy. In the continuing aftermath of pain and reproach, the poet here prays for Yahweh to remember—to intervene in covenant mercy. And the poet calls for His merciful look in the midst of reproach. The prayer asks for God's intervention and compassionate deliverance in light of His covenant promises (cf. 3:61–63; Exodus 3:7; Psalm. 74:18, 22; 89:50–51).

VERSE 2

Our inheritance has been turned over to strangers, our houses to aliens.

Israel's "inheritance" was the land promised to Abraham, Isaac, and Jacob. It may also include a reference to the temple that stood at the religious center of Israel's inheritance. Psalm 79:1 says, "O God, the nations have invaded your inheritance; they have defiled Your holy temple; they have laid Jerusalem in ruins." This is exactly what both Moses and Jeremiah wrote about as a consequence of Israel's faithlessness. Jeremiah 6:12 says, "'Their houses shall be turned over to others, their fields and their wives together; for I will stretch out My hand against the inhabitants of the land,' declares the LORD" (see also Deuteronomy 28:30). Ezekiel wrote: "I will bring the worst of the nations, and they will possess their houses…" in 7:24 (see also Amos 5:11 and Zephaniah 1:13).

Jeremiah 52:13 and 2 Kings 25:9 say that all the houses of Jerusalem were destroyed—at least every "great house."[4] But according to this verse, even the burned-out ruins that remained belonged to "aliens." This suffering hit as close to home as possible, taking even their own houses. John Calvin writes:

> For it sometimes happens, that when one loses his farm, his fields, and vineyards, his house remains to him untouched; but the Prophet here

---

4   See Kaiser, 118.

amplifies the misery of his own nation, that they were not only deprived of their fields and possessions, but that they were also ejected from their own houses, and others had possession of them.[5]

Jeremiah reminded the Lord of their reproach—"In a very real sense the land remained the property of the LORD (Leviticus 25:23). Can he rest content that his domain has fallen into the hands of others (cf. Jeremiah 12:7–13)?"[6]

VERSE 3

We have become orphans without a father, our mothers are like widows

Again Jeremiah may have been referencing Moses. Exodus 22:21–24 says:

> You shall not wrong a stranger or oppress him, for you were strangers in the land of Egypt. You shall not afflict any widow or orphan. If you afflict him at all, and if he does cry out to Me, I will surely hear his cry; and My anger will be kindled, and I will kill you with the sword, and your wives shall become widows and your children fatherless. (See also Deuteronomy 24:17; 27:19; Isaiah 1:17, 23; Jeremiah 7:6; 22:3; Ezekiel 22:7)

No doubt, many of the survivors had lost loved ones and were now orphans or widows.

Perhaps Jeremiah was speaking figuratively however[7] and likening Israel to those who were defenseless—the destitute and most vulnerable in society, without protection. Whether in a literal or figurative sense, this was true of everyone in Israel after the Babylonian siege and the destruction that followed. The survivors were helpless and unprotected from the ravages of starvation, exploitation, and the like.

---

5   John Calvin, *Calvin's Commentaries, Volume XI* (Grand Rapids: Baker Books, 2005), 494.
6   Mackay, 211.
7   See Kaiser, 119.

Verse 4

We have to pay for our drinking water, our wood comes to us at a price
Everything they had was taken away by the enemy, and they were now forced to buy it back. This is desperate poverty. Again Deuteronomy 28 seems to allude to this as part of the covenant curses: "Because you did not serve the Lord your God with joy and a glad heart, for the abundance of all things; therefore you shall serve your enemies whom the Lord will send against you, in hunger, in thirst, in nakedness, and in the lack of all things" (vv. 47–48).

The mercies of the Lord are indeed new every morning (3:23), but the harsh reality was that the remnant had to pay for their drinking water and wood—the necessities for survival.

Verse 5

Our pursuers are at our necks; we are worn out, there is no rest for us
Because the people of Israel stiffened their necks against the preaching of God's prophet, their persecutors were domineering over them, constantly on their necks. "We are worn out" means they were completely exhausted from the stress. One writer says, "Persecution and fear dogged their every footstep."[8] There was no peace or rest, just intense pressure.

Deuteronomy 12:10 and 25:19 (among other places) speak of God promising rest to Israel when they entered the land. But because of their idolatry, there was now no rest for the remnant. Note the irony of Jeremiah's previous ministry in Jeremiah 17:19–27. Because Israel had chosen to treat their God-ordained rest with contempt, they had no rest. As Guest writes: "Against the appeal of Jeremiah, the people insisted on making the Sabbath one more day of getting and spending. Now they paid the inexorable price. They got what they wanted and found it to be a horror"[9] (see also Deuteronomy 28:48b; 65–67).

---

8   Charles H. Dyer, "Lamentations," in John F. Walvoord and Roy B. Zuck, eds., *The Bible Knowledge Commentary* (Wheaton: Victor Books, 1985), 1222.
9   John Guest, *Mastering the Old Testament: Jeremiah, Lamentations* vol. 17 (Nashville: Word, 1988), 386.

VERSE 6

We have submitted to Egypt and Assyria to get enough bread

The Hebrew reads: "Egypt we gave a hand and Assyria for satisfaction of bread." It is possible to understand this enigmatic phrase as a reference to Jewish exiles in Egypt and Assyria begging for bread.[10] But the language and following context better fits with preexilic alliances in Israel's past, for the sake of prosperity. To "give the hand" is used at times of a pledge or agreement (see Ezra 10:19; Jeremiah 50:15; Ezekiel 17:18). This could then speak of political alliances for the sake of economic gain or religious alliances with their gods (also for the sake of economic gain). Either way, the sin of faithlessness is what is being confessed. Judah shifted her loyalty away from an omnipotent God and toward the strength of godless nations. They went to Egypt and Assyria—two nations that had already proven themselves godless in their treatment of Israel—because they did not trust God. They went to these nations not only for financial aid, but also for love of the nations' idols. Jeremiah had rebuked Israel in Jeremiah 2:18–19, 36:

> "But now what are you doing on the road to Egypt, to drink the waters of the Nile? Or what are you doing on the road to Assyria, to drink the waters of the Euphrates? Your own wickedness will correct you, and your apostasies will reprove you; know therefore and see that it is evil and bitter for you to forsake the LORD your God, and the dread of Me is not in you," declares the Lord God of hosts.… "Also, you will be put to shame by Egypt as you were put to shame by Assyria."

See also Isaiah 30:1–7a; 31:1–3; Ezekiel 16:26–28; 23:12, 21; Hosea 5:13; 7:11; 9:3; 12:1 (cf. Jeremiah 44:12–14).

VERSE 7

Our fathers sinned, and are no more; it is we who have borne their iniquities

According to Jeremiah 31:29 and Ezekiel 18:2, there was a proverb among the Jews: "The fathers eat the sour grapes, but the children's teeth are set on

---

10 See Mackay, 213–14; cf. Deuteronomy 28:48.

edge." But Jeremiah had warned Israel that everyone would "die for his own iniquity; each man who eats the sour grapes, his teeth will be set on edge" (Jeremiah 31:30). Ezekiel devoted an entire chapter to the justice of the judgment of God and a call to repent (Ezekiel 18; see also Exodus 34:7 and Deuteronomy 5:9).

It is true however that the "fathers" had indeed "sinned." It was because of the sin of Manasseh that judgment would come (2 Kings 23:26; 24:3). Yet the "iniquities" of Jeremiah's generation hastened the cup. In Jeremiah 3:25 he wrote: "Let us lie down in our shame, and let our humiliation cover us; for we have sinned against the LORD our God, *we and our fathers*, from our youth even to this day. And we have not obeyed the voice of the LORD our God" (see also Jeremiah 16:11–13). Lamentations itself has been quite clear about who had sinned (cf. 1:5, 8, 9, 14, 18; 2:14; 3:42; 4:6, 12–14)—note 5:16: "Woe to us, for we have sinned!"

VERSE 8

Slaves rule over us; there is no one to deliver us from their hand

Serious role reversal had taken place within their society. The slaves now ruled over them. Once again, Deuteronomy 28 alluded to these consequences some eight centuries prior: "The alien who is among you shall rise above you higher and higher, but you will go down lower and lower. He shall lend to you, but you will not lend to him; he shall be the head, and you will be the tail" (vv. 43–44; see also v. 48). Proverbs 30:21–22 says that the rule of a slave is unbearable: "Under three things the earth quakes, and under four, it cannot bear up: Under a slave when he becomes king..." (cf. Proverbs 19:10; Ecclesiastes 10:6–7). "Judah is no longer ruled by an independent king in Jerusalem, but by the underlings of a foreign emperor. Alternatively, this verse may refer to the land as placed under the control of those from surrounding nations who had once been Judah's vassals, probably the Edomites (cf. 4:21)."[11]

"No one" could "deliver" Israel "from their hand" because God had ordained it, and as Isaiah 43:13 says, "There is none who can deliver out of [His] hand; [He acts] and who can reverse it?"

---

11 Mackay, 215.

Verse 9

We get our bread at the risk of our lives / because of the sword in the wilderness

Jeremiah 41:8 includes an interesting note about hidden supplies after the destruction of Jerusalem. Burying treasure and valuables was a common practice during war. But marauding bandits—perhaps either Babylonians or Arab Bedouins—evidently would plunder any of the rescued valuables, or even the first meager harvests the remnant tried to live on. Deuteronomy 28:33 is again the prophetic backdrop for this painful reality, "A people whom you do not know shall eat up the produce of your ground and all your labors, and you will never be anything but oppressed and crushed continually."

Verse 10

Our skin has become as hot as an oven, because of the burning heat of famine

Severe fever arose from the famine. In 4:8, the prophet wrote: "Their appearance is blacker than soot, they are not recognized in the streets; their skin is shriveled on their bones, it is withered, it has become like wood." Job 30:30 reads: "My skin turns black on me, and my bones burn with fever."

In verses 1–10, the poet uses the plural pronouns to speak for the remnant in prayer. It was a continued prayer for mercy while enduring all kinds of suffering. This was their reproach. The city once famous for its reflection of the glory of God is now known by these wretched descriptions. Therefore, their confession of faith is: "Lord, remember us. Remember our reproach. Turn to us. Look to us. Come to our aid. Have compassion on us."

Verse 11

They ravished the women in Zion, the virgins in the cities of Judah

In verses 11–14, Jeremiah moves to a third person description rather than a corporate use of the pronouns *we, our,* and *us* as he describes how the consequences of Judah's rebellion touched all segments of society. No one was spared when the Babylonians took the city.

Here the prophet tells the Lord of the horrors that were suffered—in particular the rape of the women, both married and unmarried, in Jerusalem and Judah. Again this was in keeping with the covenant curses listed in Deuteronomy 28:30a: "You shall betroth a wife, but another man will violate her."

VERSE 12

Princes were hung by their hands; elders were not respected

This could refer to either torture or death. Zedekiah's sons and all the nobles were executed, according to Jeremiah 39:6. Thus their bodies may have been "hung by their hands," or they may have been "hung by their hands" before they were put to death. It is also possible, though perhaps less likely grammatically, for the phrase "by their hands" to refer to the Chaldeans—the Babylonians executed the "princes" of Judah via the ignoble and accursed death of hanging.

The second statement is literally, "The faces of the elders were not respected." This is likely a reference to the deliberate shaming of those who were normally respected and honored in Israel.[12]

VERSE 13

Young men worked at the grinding mill, and youths stumbled under loads of wood

Working at the "grinding mill" and carrying "loads of wood" were tasks normally reserved for the lowest of slaves (Joshua 9:27; Judges 16:21). Israel's children did the work normally performed by animals or slaves. They "worked at the grinding mill," turning the millstones like Samson was forced to do after the Philistines plucked out his eyes (Judges 16:21). Deuteronomy 28:50 speaks of a conquering nation with a fierce countenance "who will have no respect for the old, nor show favor to the young."

---

12 H. L. Ellison, "Lamentations," in *The Expositor's Bible Commentary*, ed. Frank E. Gaebelein (Grand Rapids: Zondervan, 1986), 731.

Verse 14

Elders are gone from the gate, young men from their music

"Elders" at "the gate" would normally conduct business as well as dispense justice and wisdom (Joshua 20:4; Ruth 4:1ff; cf. Job 29:7–17 for an example of the "gate of the city" in an ancient near east culture). Their very source of wisdom and experience was no longer available because their spiritual leaders were grieving as well. Israel's economy, justice, and way of life were gone because of sin and its consequences. Lamentations 2:10 says this: "The elders of the daughter of Zion sit on the ground, they are silent. They have thrown dust on their heads; They have girded themselves with sackcloth." Young men are kept "from their music." The joy that once characterized this city of God had ceased; it had turned to deep sorrow. Jeremiah had warned Israel of this in Jeremiah 7:34 and 16:9. "For thus says the LORD of hosts, the God of Israel: 'Behold, I am going to eliminate from this place, before your eyes and in your time, the voice of rejoicing and the voice of gladness, the voice of the groom and the voice of the bride'" (Jeremiah 16:9).

Verse 15

The joy of our hearts has ceased; our dancing has been turned into mourning

The prophet Amos foreshadowed this type of turnaround when he predicted the earlier Assyrian exile:

> Those who recline on beds of ivory and sprawl on their couches, and eat lambs from the flock and calves from the midst of the stall, who improvise to the sound of the harp, and like David have composed songs for themselves, who drink wine from sacrificial bowls while they anoint themselves with the finest of oils, yet they have not grieved over the ruin of Joseph. Therefore they will now go into exile at the head of the exiles, and the sprawlers' banqueting will pass away.... Then I will turn your festivals into mourning and all your songs into lamentation; And I will bring sackcloth on everyone's loins and baldness on every head. And I will make it like a time of mourning for an only son, and the end of it will be like a bitter day. (Amos 6:4–7; 8:10)

What was true in the northern kingdom was now true in Judah and Jerusalem. Note contrast with Psalm 30:11. Psalm 149:3 exhorts the Israelite worshippers: "Let them praise His name with dancing…." Psalm 15:4 reads: "Praise Him with timbrel and dancing…." But such displays of joyous worship are now gone, as utter destitution and tragedy had come upon God's chosen people. In fact, "mourning" had now taken its place.

VERSE 16

The crown has fallen from our head; woe to us, for we have sinned!

"The crown" here seems to speak metaphorically of that which was an honor to Israel (see Job 19:9; Jeremiah 13:18; Ezekiel 21:25–26). Included would be its walled city. Psalm 89:38–40 says, "But You have cast off and rejected, You have been full of wrath against Your anointed. You have spurned the covenant of Your servant; You have profaned his crown in the dust. You have broken down all his walls; You have brought his strongholds to ruin." As well, the literal crown of Israel, her king, ceased to have any authority and was removed from office. The Davidic dynasty was now destined for obscurity until the time of Christ. The word *woe* expresses a deep sense of grief—in this case because "we have sinned," that is the people of Israel in Jeremiah's day.

VERSE 17

Because of this our heart is faint, because of these things our eyes are dim

Their hearts were faint, or unwell. The inner person was shriveling up from grief and despair. The prophet had written in Jeremiah 4:18: "Your ways and your deeds have brought these things to you. This is your evil. How bitter! How it has touched your heart!" The prophet knew that pain as well, in Jeremiah 8:18 he wrote: "My sorrow is beyond healing, my heart is faint within me!" Lamentations 1:22b says, "For my groans are many and my heart is faint" (see also 1:13d). The remnants' "eyes are dim" due to weeping over the horrible condition of Jerusalem. The comparison with 2:11 here illustrates the same truth, but note the different tone of the two chapters (see Job 17:7; Psalm 6:7; 31:9; 69:3 for the same type of language). This was predicted in Deuteronomy 28:65–66:

"Among those nations you shall find no rest, and there will be no resting place for the sole of your foot; but there the LORD will give you a trembling heart, failing of eyes, and despair of soul. So your life shall hang in doubt before you; and you will be in dread night and day, and shall have no assurance of your life." Moses warned them that if they rebelled against the Lord and worshiped false gods, they should expect to be taken captive to a place where there would be no rest. Instead, they would experience sickness of heart, which is exactly what happened.

VERSE 18

Because of Mount Zion which lies desolate, foxes prowl in it.

The reason for their sorrow is the desolation of "Mount Zion"—the destruction of the temple, perhaps including the entire city of Jerusalem. "Foxes" now "prowl in it" instead of prophets, priests, and kings. Though the KJV reads "jackals" here instead of "foxes," the Hebrew word differs from the one used in 4:3. The point is obvious, whichever the exact animal—the place where the true and living God once symbolically sat enthroned among men was now desolate. The wild animals made it their home. God had warned Solomon that if the people did not walk with God, but turned to idolatry, this would happen: "And this house will become a heap of ruins; everyone who passes by will be astonished and hiss and say, 'why has the LORD done thus to this land and to this house?'" (1 Kings 9:8).

VERSE 19

You, O LORD, rule forever; your throne is from generation to generation

Jeremiah now turns to direct address as he calls on Yahweh as the all-sovereign ruler. Literally he says: "You, Yahweh, sit forever." Psalm 102:12 uses the same phrase in a similar context of seeking compassion upon Zion: "But You, O LORD, abide forever, and Your name to all generations" (cf. Psalm 102).

Even though the temple was desolate, Yahweh still sits forever enthroned "from generation to generation." He had seen it all. In fact, He was the One who had caused her calamity. How could they possibly escape His notice when He, in His loving hand of discipline, had caused their affliction to bring them back to Himself? The language of an abiding "throne" is also very similar to messianic passages such as 2 Samuel 7:16 and Psalm 45:6 (cf. Hebrews 1:8–9). No doubt, being steeped in the promises of the Old Testament, the prophet was alluding to not only God's sovereignty, but also His messianic promises. As Jeremiah confirms Yahweh's sovereignty, he reconnects with the only true ground of hope. As we have repeatedly seen in the book of Lamentations, every time that Jeremiah and his people are brought to their lowest point, God redirects their focus to Him.

Yet questions remained in light of the horrible plight God's chosen nation was enduring.

Verse 20

Why do You forget us forever? Why do you forsake us so long?
Even though the songwriter embraced Yahweh's mercy and love in chapter 3, the aftermath of day in and day out dealing with ongoing pain and grief was very real. The remnant knew God ruled forever. They knew that His throne endures forever and His promises are faithful. *Yet the pain still seemed to go on and on.* Thus, as a spokesman for the remnant, he asks, "Why do You forget us forever? Why do you forsake us so long?" Psalm 79:5 asks in a similar context: "How long, O LORD? Will You be angry forever? Will Your jealousy burn like fire?" Perhaps the New Testament plea—"I do believe; help my unbelief" (Mark 9:24)—reveals the same heart struggle.

This leads the writer full circle to his original plea in verse 1. It felt like God had forgotten, thus he prayed, "Remember." It felt that God had forsaken, thus he prayed, "Look and see." But the writer persevered, as the next verse indicates.

Verse 21

Restore us to You, O LORD, that we may be restored; renew our days as of old
The prophet—speaking for the remnant—says, "Turn us, Yahweh, unto You, and we will be turned." This is a prayer for both repentance and restoration. In essence, their cry is, "Lord, bring us back to You. Your discipline has accomplished

its purpose. We want to come back to you." The phrase "to You" reveals that this is more than just a desire for a restored nation and restored personal comforts. This is a prayer for restored fellowship with God. Only in Yahweh would they find solace. Mackay aptly points out, however:

> But repentance itself is dependent on the gift of God, who alone can grant the repentance which leads to life (cf. Acts 11:18; 2 Timothy 2:25). So there is a recognition that, because they have not the capacity to effect the renewal and restoration themselves, they cannot begin to step out on the road towards reconciliation unless there is a divinely granted predisposition and empowerment.[13]

Moreover, this prayer also recalls the promise of Deuteronomy 4:30–31: "When you are in distress and all these things have come upon you, in the latter days you will return to the LORD your God and listen to His voice. For the LORD your God is a compassionate God; He will not fail you nor destroy you nor forget the covenant with your fathers which He swore to them" (see also Deuteronomy 30:1–10; Jeremiah 30:18–20; 31:18–20; 32:39–40). The phrase, "renew our days as of old," shares the same Hebrew term here translated "as of old" with Jeremiah 30:20, which references Yahweh's promise of restoration—that the descendants of Israel would be as "formerly"—or "as of old". Thus, verse 21 is a plea for Yahweh's covenant grace in fulfilling His promises of restoration.

After asking for repentance and restoration, the poet, speaking for the remnant, asks God to remember His covenant promises—but in a way that captures the fear and frailty of a people who finally and fully recognize their utter poverty of spirit.

VERSE 22

Unless You have utterly rejected us / and are exceedingly angry with us
Jewish liturgy actually repeats verse 21 after verse 22. But the Holy Spirit inspired verse 22 as the final verse of the book. Though it seems to have a rather negative, anticlimactic ending, it actually is a cry of hope. The grammar is difficult here,

---

13 Mackay, 224.

but it seems best to understand verse 22 as an explanatory clause that is related to verse 21: "Restore us, O LORD...renew our days of old—unless You have utterly rejected and are exceedingly angry with us." The implication is that the remnant feels utterly rejected, but they can't fathom that God would actually break His covenant. The sentence expects a negative answer—"surely rejecting, You haven't rejected us, have You?" Even though they rebelled against Him and were severely chastened, God will not reject them. Instead, He will restore them. The Scriptures are replete with promises that God would never ultimately abandon His people. Leviticus 26:44, in the context of the covenant curses, says this: "Yet in spite of this, when they are in the land of their enemies, I will not reject them, nor will I so abhor them as to destroy them, breaking My covenant with them; for I am the LORD their God." Even Jeremiah himself wrote of the promise of the New Covenant in Jeremiah 31:31–37. But here we see the remnant stripped bare—they realize that God owes them nothing. The promises of restoration in Deuteronomy 30 are a gift—not something to be demanded.

Verse 22 ends with a whimper—"unless You have utterly rejected us"—but there is faith embedded in such a whimper. All religious presumption is gone. Finally, and gloriously—mercy can be rightly received and appreciated. God's Word confirms that He would not utterly reject Israel for the sake of His promises to Abraham, Isaac, and Jacob.

INSIGHTS FOR COUNSELING

In ending Lamentations the way He did, the Holy Spirit was helping a brutalized remnant cope with long-lasting grief and pain. Even though faith is affirmed, the pain still exists. When we finally come to the point of accepting the woeful consequences sin has brought into our lives, we are tempted to think that we now must trudge through life on our own, in our own strength. Yes, God has forgiven us. We accept that. We know we have received His mercy. But we often think that now it is up to us to make sense of whatever life remains. After all, we made the mess; now it is up to us to clean it up.

Certainly one of the purposes of God's discipline is to cause us to face life responsibly, but there is a fine line between becoming responsible and becoming self-sufficient. What we really need is to be trained to depend on the Lord through continual prayer—to *continue* to cry out to the Lord to remember, to look, and to see. To *continue* to recount the sad situation to Him. To *continue* to reveal the consequences of sin and confession of sin to Him. And finally, to *continue* to affirm His sovereign rule and seek His restoration and renewal—even if it doesn't seem humanly possible. Knowing the freshness of His mercies, and the greatness of His faithfulness, we must cry out to God to dispense these to us in appropriate portions according to our need.

He will always be true to His promises. "Blessed are the poor in spirit, for theirs is the kingdom of heaven. Blessed are those who mourn, for they shall be comforted" (Matthew 5:3–4). Jesus is the God who was faithful to bring the covenant curses—and He will be faithful to His promises of blessing. The poor in spirit will inherit the kingdom, and those who mourn will be comforted. When, by faith, we embrace our own poverty of spirit—and the truth that man has no right to demand anything from God—there is an overriding conviction and hope for the presence of God. He is a rewarder of those who diligently seek Him (Hebrews 11:6b). "To this one I will look, to him who is humble and contrite of spirit, and who trembles at My word" (Isaiah 66:2b). God gives grace to the humble but resists the proud (Proverbs 3:34; James 4:6; 1 Petet 5:5). Lamentations calls the sufferer to humility and, thus, grace. Consequently, there are a number of principles for us to consider.

1. We must come to the conclusion that God's sovereignty rules over all.

Psalm 103:19 is crystal clear: "The Lord has established His throne in the heavens, and His sovereignty rules over all." God's sovereignty *includes* all the suffering we experience, no matter how deep, whether it is caused by our own sin, another person's sin, or simply the result of living in a sin-cursed world. There is no hope anywhere else. King Nebuchadnezzar was forced to come to this conclusion concerning God's sovereignty. After exalting himself to be the king of the earth, Nebuchadnezzar was put out to pasture by God for seven years so that he acted like a grazing cow until he recognized that the God of heaven alone is sovereign.

Then the king said, "But at the end of that period, I, Nebuchadnezzar, raised my eyes toward heaven and my reason returned to me, and I blessed the Most High and praised and honored Him who lives forever; for His dominion is an everlasting dominion, and His kingdom endures from generation to generation" (Daniel 4:34). It is God's sovereignty that gives us hope in the midst of our suffering. Walter Kaiser writes, "All else may change, but He changes not. God's throne and rule over all things is thoroughly opposed to what men call chance or blind fate. Everything may fluctuate, men and times may grow harder and more difficult, but God still remains in charge of the situation."[14] We need to be able to say with Jeremiah, "You, O Lord, rule forever. There is nothing that escapes Your notice. There is nothing that is not part of Your good purpose" (Lamentations 5:19; Romans 8:28).

2. Repentance is a 180-degree turn away from sin, to God.

Both elements are required. Some people try to find repentance by just turning away from sin. They refuse to also bow to God. They want to find a repentance of their own, which is not repentance but a penance they prescribe for themselves. There they are stuck because they will not lift their eyes to heaven—to God. It is not enough to turn from sin. We must also *turn to* God in obedient faith. Penance is sinward and self-centered. True repentance is Godward and Christ-centered. Charles Spurgeon said, "He who looks sinward has his back to God—he who looks Godward has his back to sin."[15] Restoration of fellowship with God requires distaste for our sin and an appetite for obedience. We are not ready to receive the fullness of God's mercy until we are humble enough to recognize how desperately we need it. We are not ready to turn our backs on the sin we cherish until we are ready to turn our faces toward a singular devotion to God (Lamentations 5:1, 16, 21a; Psalm 24:1–6; 66:18–20).

3. When sorrow continues, though softened by the comfort of faith and hope, we must continue to seek God's mercy

We must continue to ask that He would "remember" and "see" according to His Word. We can also tell Him of our ongoing reproach, as verses 2–10 reveal. After we have embraced the Lord's sovereignty and lovingkindness, we often still face devastating temporal consequences. We can do so with a *continued prayer for mercy* and an account before the Lord of our sad situation (Lamentations 5:2–10, 19–20; 1 Chronicles 16:11; Psalm 27:7–9; Hosea 5:15).

---

14 Walter C. Kaiser, *Grief & Pain in the Plan of God* (Fearn: Christian Focus, 2004), 116.
15 Cited in Kerry James Allen, *Exploring the Mind & Heart of the Prince of Preachers* (Oswego, IL: Fox River Press, 2005), 385.

4. Sin promises fullness, happiness, and glory.

But in the end, it brings emptiness, sadness, and humiliation. The prophet sang of what was lost because of sin—*the gate was empty; the gaiety was gone;* and *the glory was gone.* Sin brings loss of wisdom, loss of joy, and loss of honor. Sin brings the fear of judgment and faintness of heart. Sin brings sorrow and a soiled testimony to the truth about God's glory (Lamentations 5:12–16; Proverbs 28:1; Psalm 32:3-4).

5. Prayer does not immediately bring relief from the feelings that follow in the wake of sin's consequences.

Sometimes, even after one has prayed, the feelings of loneliness and abandonment remain. Here, the endurance of our faith is tested to the extreme. But we must cling to the truths we know. If we are believers in Jesus Christ, God has made an irrevocable covenant with us. He is more committed to us than we are to Him. No suffering—even pain that defies description—can ever separate us from His love and undying mercy (Lamentations 5:21–22; Romans 8:31–39).

HOMEWORK FOR COUNSELING

You are encouraged to photocopy homework pages for use in personal counseling.

PART 1: THINKING RIGHTLY ABOUT SIN AND ABOUT GOD

1. Jeremiah prayed, "Remember, O LORD, what has befallen us; look, and see our reproach!" (5:1). Then he recited the reproaches of God's people. List every reproach you presently experience as the result of sin.

2. It is sometimes true that we suffer consequences from the sins of our parents (Exodus 20:5). However, this is never justification for blame shifting. Each of us is responsible for our own sins before God. In what ways might you be blaming others, particularly your parents, for "the way you are"? Confess this blame shifting to God, and tell Him you will take full ownership of your sin from this point forward.

3. The point of the book of Lamentations will be lost if the grief and sorrow we experience from sin do not drive us to restoration with God.

"Restore us to You, O LORD, that we may be restored" must be our prayer (5:21). What practical steps must you take to experience full restoration with God? Where are you on the 180-degree turn from sin and back to God? How will you move forward from here?

4.   Pray through Psalm 143, confessing specific sins as needed, asking God to help you and to teach you to walk in His ways.

PART 2: HOPING IN JESUS

My friend, we don't know the tragedy sin has brought into your life, but God knows. God knows all the sins you have committed against Him and all the sins others have committed against you. And He stands ready to forgive, ready to heal, ready to receive, and ready to walk with you through the pain of facing your sin as you look to the One who died to grant you new life. In this book, we have seen the effects of sin in perhaps more potent ways than ever before. The question each of us must ask is, "Am I sick of my sin yet?" We won't go to the doctor until we recognize we need one. We won't go to the One who can heal our soul, the lover of our soul, until we are really sick of our sin.

The promise of God is sure. If we will come to Him in repentant faith, if we will trust His work of redemption, He will accept us in Christ Jesus. If we repent of our sin and believe in Christ, He will forgive us. This is not penance. This is receiving the gift of God's grace. God will heal us, all because of Christ. Ephesians 1:7 says, "In Him [Jesus Christ] we have redemption through His blood, the forgiveness of our trespasses, according to the riches of His grace." Will you turn to Him today? Will you go to Him for mercy? This study of sin, its consequences, and the corresponding grief it brings into our lives must drive us to the Cross of Christ or it will not accomplish the purpose for which God sent it. There is no hope anywhere else. Run to the Cross of Jesus as fast as you can. Respond to His invitation: "Come to Me, all who are weary and heavy-laden, and I will give you rest. Take My yoke upon you and learn from Me, for I am gentle and humble in heart, and YOU WILL FIND REST FOR YOUR SOULS. For My yoke is easy and My burden is light" (Matthew 11:28–30). In Him, and Him alone, you will receive mercy.

STUDY GUIDE

CHAPTER 1 — LAMENTATIONS 1:1–22

1. Read 2 Kings 25:1–21. Discuss the fall of Jerusalem to Nebuchadnezzar, king of Babylon.

2. Read Jeremiah 25:1–14. Why did God judge Judah with seventy years of captivity? What are some of the sin causes?

3. Read Jeremiah 2:29–30; 5:3–6; 5:20–25; 6:10. What was Judah's atti-
    tude toward God's Word and His correction? What words would you
    use to describe your attitude toward the preaching of God's Word? Do
    you faithfully sit under the consistent preaching of the Bible?

4. Read Hebrews 12:3–11. Why does God discipline His children? What
    is His intended purpose in the suffering He ordains? Compare with
    James 1:2–4. How submissive are you to God's discipline? Are you will-
    ingly trained by it, or do you bemoan it?

5. Read Psalm 34:18 and Isaiah 66:2. What can we be assured of in the
    midst of our affliction?

6. How does your thinking need to change about sin and about God?

7. Read the following Scriptures: 2 Corinthians 5:21; 1 Peter 2:24–25; 3:18; Hebrews 10:19–25; 1 John 1:8–2:2. How did the atoning work of Jesus on the cross open the way to God? Are you trusting in Him alone to make you right with God? Take time in prayer to confess this and thank God for the forgiveness that belongs to those who trust in Christ.

8. Who do you know that is going through a time of intense grief and suffering? What can you do this week to show that person that someone cares? How can you redirect his or her focus to God? If, to your knowledge, the grief and suffering is caused by sin, in what ways can you exhort him or her to repent and return to the Lord?

Chapter 2 — Lamentations 2:1–22

1. Read 2 Chronicles 36:1–21. Discuss the fall of Jerusalem to Nebuchadnezzar, king of Babylon. Compare this historical account with what James 1:14–15 teaches about the "process" of sin.

2. Look up the following Scriptures. Chart what they teach concerning the anger of God. What provokes God's anger? What attributes of God are revealed? Exodus 32:1–10; Numbers 16:1–50; Psalm 7:11; Jeremiah 25:15–29; John 3:36; Revelation 19:12–15

3. How does your thinking need to change about sin and about God? Pray Psalm 32 back to God, confessing specific sins as needed and thanking God for His forgiveness.

4. Meditate on Psalm 77. Especially note the feelings of grief and despair revealed in verses 7–10. In light of these, what is the significance of the psalmist's decision in verse 11?

5. Look up the following Scriptures. What relationship does Jesus have to the anger of God the Father? John 8:11; Matthew 26:36–46; Romans 3:25–26; Romans 5:6–10; 1 Thessalonians 1:10

6. Who do you know that is going through a time of intense grief and suffering? What can you do this week to show that person that someone cares? How can you redirect his or her focus to God? If, to your knowledge, the grief and suffering is caused by sin, in what ways can you exhort him or her to repent and return to the Lord?

7. Who do you know that is an unbeliever and therefore remains under the wrath of God? How can you reach out to them with the good news that Jesus drank the cup of God's wrath?

CHAPTER 3 — LAMENTATIONS 3:1–18

1. Read Deuteronomy 29:16–19. What did God warn Israel against? What did He say would happen if His people lived in disobedience? Compare this to the experience of Naomi in Ruth 1:19–21.

2. Read Isaiah 6:1–8. Describe Isaiah's vision of the Lord. How did a renewed view of God's holiness affect Isaiah?

3. Read James 4:1–10. What forms of worldliness do you find in this passage? How is pride related to them? In light of verse 6, what does it mean for a believer to be a "practical enemy of God"?

4. Read Romans 5:1–5. Discuss biblical hope. What is hope? Where is it found?

5. Read Ephesians 1:1–12. What does it mean to be accepted by God?

6. Read out loud Mark 15:1–47. Consider the suffering Jesus endured as He took our sins upon Himself. Give thanks to God in prayer for His great love displayed on the Cross of Calvary.

CHAPTER 4—LAMENTATIONS 3:19-39

1. Read Nehemiah 9:1–38. What do you learn about the mercy, patience, compassion, and faithfulness of God toward Israel?

2. Read Genesis 37–50. As you read, note the situations Joseph found himself in that were completely out of his control. Reflect on his response to his brothers in 50:20. Compare this with Romans 8:28. What are some reasons we can trust our sovereign God in the midst of affliction?

CHAPTER 5 — LAMENTATIONS 3:40-66

1. When Nebuchadnezzar conquered Jerusalem, the prophet Daniel was taken captive to Babylon while he was still a young man, probably in his teen years. Many years later, under the reign of Darius, Daniel was reading Jeremiah and noticed the prophecy that clearly predicted the desolation of Jerusalem and defined the length of the captivity as being seventy years (Daniel 9:1–3). This led Daniel to fast and pray for the repentance of God's people. As a spiritual leader and representative of God's people, he then prayed a prayer of confession to God. Read this prayer in Daniel 9:4–19.

   • In what ways had the people sinned?

   • What attributes of God are revealed?

   • What consequences of sin are mentioned?

   • What characteristics of biblical confession are evidenced here?

   • What do we learn from this model prayer?]

2. How will you pray differently as a result of having studied Daniel's prayer?

3. What specific sins is the Holy Spirit convicting you of? Will you repent of them? What evidences of repentance can you expect to see in your life?

4. Study Psalm 102. What does it teach you about your sin and about God?

5. After studying the psalm, pray through this passage of Scripture, confessing specific sins as needed, asking God for His help, and thanking Him for His kindness and forgiveness.

Chapter 6 — Lamentations 4:1-22

1. Read 2 Samuel 12:1–23. What motivated Nathan to confront David? What principles of loving confrontation can you glean from Nathan's example? Discuss David's response. Compare his response to Psalm 51, the psalm typically attributed to this time period in David's life.

2. Read James 5:13–18. What relationship might personal sin have to physical suffering? Discuss the significance of the phrase "confess your sins to one another." When and how is this kind of confession appropriate? Are there any dangers to be aware of?

3. Read Psalm 130. What does this psalm reveal concerning a proper attitude toward sin? What qualities of God does the psalmist affirm as he finds hope in divine grace and forgiveness?

4. Read 1 John 1:8–2:2. Discuss the connection between the phrases "He
    is faithful and righteous," "we have an advocate," and "He Himself
    is our propitiation." Propitiation means satisfaction. How did Jesus
    appease God's wrath and satisfy His righteous demands? Compare with
    Romans 3:25, Hebrews 2:17, and 1 John 4:10.

CHAPTER 7 — LAMENTATIONS 5:1-22

1. Read through Deuteronomy 28, where Moses warns the nation of Israel about the consequences of disobeying God. Make note of which curses came true in the historical setting of the book of Lamentations.

2. Read Deuteronomy 30, where Moses promises Israel that God will restore her when she is willing to repent and return to the Lord. What evidences of repentance do you find in this passage?

3. Read Galatians 3:13. What does it mean that Jesus became a curse for us? Read Romans 5:20–21. How does the grace of God in Jesus Christ free believers from the curse of the Law?

4. Make a list of the biblical principles you have learned from this study of the book of Lamentations. For example:

- Rebellion always carries a high price tag.

- There is no hope for the man or woman who refuses to repent.

5. Considering all the lessons the Holy Spirit has taught you through studying the book of Lamentations, write out your own one-page responsive prayer to the Lord.

SELECTED BIBLIOGRAPHY

Constable, Thomas L. *Expository Notes on the Bible*. Garland, TX: Galaxie Software.

Dyer, Charles H. "Lamentations" in *The Bible Knowledge Commentary*. ed. by Walvoord, John F. and Zuck, Roy B. Victor Books, 1985.

Ellison, H.L. "Lamentations" in *The Expositor's Bible Commentary*. ed. by Gaebelein, Frank E. Grand Rapids: Zondervan, 1986.

Guest, John. *Mastering the Old Testament: Jeremiah, Lamentations*. Vol. 17. Word, 1988. Occasionally useful for quotes or synthesis.

Harrison, R.K. *Jeremiah & Lamentations*. Downers Grove, IL: IVP, 1973. Helpful at times for theological synthesis and explanation.

Horton, Stanley M. "Lamentations" in *The Complete Biblical Library*. Springfield: World Library Press, 2000.

Jensen, Irving L. *Jeremiah and Lamentations* (Everyman's Bible Commentary). Chicago: Moody, 1974. Brief survey, but helpful at points for the purpose of overview and synthesis.

Kaiser, Walter C. Jr. *Grief & Pain in the Plan of God*. Fearn: Christian Focus, 2004. This is by far the most suggestive resource for preaching through the book of Lamentations. Along with Mackay's more detailed exegetical work, it is a must for the preacher and teacher.

Laetsch, Theo. *Jeremiah*. St. Louis: Concordia, 1952.

Mackay, John L. Lamentations: A Mentor Commentary. Fearn: Christian Focus, 2008. This is an indispensable work for the expositor.

Nagelsbach, Carl Wilhelm Eduard. "Lamentations" in *Lange's Commentary on the Holy Scriptures*. Grand Rapids: Zondervan, 1980. Difficult to read, but helpful at times.

Price, Ross. "Lamentations" in *The Wycliffe Bible Commentary*. ed. by Pfeiffer, Charles. Chicago: Moody Press, 1962.

Streane, A.W. "Jeremiah and Lamentations" in *Cambridge Bible for Schools and Colleges*. London: Cambridge University Press, 1952. Surprisingly helpful for cross-references and an occasional insight on the text.

Wiersbe, Warren W. "Lamentations" in The Bible Exposition Commentary: The Prophets. Colorado Springs: Cook Communications, 2002. Wiersbe is always insightful in packaging the text and often good for helpful quotes.

ESSENTIAL READING
FOR BIBLICAL COUNSELORS

Adams, Jay E., *Christ and Your Problems* (Phillipsburg, NJ: P&R, 1971).

——*The Christian Counselor's Manual* (Grand Rapids, MI: Zondervan, 1973).

——*Competent to Counsel* (Grand Rapids, MI: Zondervan, 1970).

——*A Theology of Counseling* (Grand Rapids, MI: Zondervan, 1979).

——(ed.) *The Journal of Modern Ministry* (2004–2008).

Baxter, Richard, *The Reformed Pastor* (1656; 1974, Edinburgh: Banner of Truth).

Berg, Jim, *Changed Into His Image* (Greenville, SC: Bob Jones University Press, 2000).

Bobgan, Martin and Deidre, *How to Counsel from Scripture* (Chicago: Moody Press, 1985).

Brauns, Chris. *Unpacking Forgiveness* (Wheaton: Crossway, 2008).

Bridges, Charles, *The Christian Ministry* (1830; 1967, Edinburgh: Banner of Truth).

Bridges, Jerry, *The Gospel for Real Life* (Colorado Springs, CO: NavPress, 2003).

——*The Discipline of Grace* (Colorado Springs, CO: NavPress, 2006).

——*The Practice of Godliness* (Colorado Springs, CO: NavPress, 1983).

——*The Pursuit of Holiness* (Colorado Springs, CO: NavPress, 1978).

——*Trusting God* (Colorado Springs, CO: NavPress, 1988).

Bulkley, Ed, *Why Christians Can't Trust Psychology* (Eugene, OR: Harvest House, 1993).

DeMoss, Nancy Leigh, *Lies Women Believe* (Chicago: Moody Press, 2001).

Fitzpatrick, Elyse, and Hendricksen, M.D., Laura, *Will Medicine Stop the Pain?* (Chicago: Moody Press, 2006).

——and Carol Cornish, (eds.), *Women Helping Women* (Eugene, OR: Harvest House, 1997).

Gallagher, Steve, *At the Altar of Sexual Idolatry* (Dry Ridge, KY: Pure Life Ministries, 2000).

Hughes, Barbara, *Disciplines of a Godly Woman* (Wheaton, IL: Crossway, 2001).

Hughes, R. Kent, *Disciplines of a Godly Man* (Wheaton, IL: Crossway, 1991).

Hull, Bill, *The Disciple Making Pastor* (Grand Rapids, MI: Fleming H. Revell, 1988).

Johnson, Eric L., and Jones, Stanton L., (eds.), *Psychology and Christianity: Four Views* (Downers Grove, IL: IVP Academic, 2000).

Jones, Robert. *Uprooting Anger* (Phillipsburg, NJ: P&R, 2005).

Lane, Timothy S., and Tripp, Paul David, *How People Change* (Winston-Salem, NC: Punch Press, 2006).

Lloyd-Jones, D. Martyn, *Spiritual Depression: Its Causes and Cure* (Grand Rapids, MI: Eerdmans, 1965).

MacArthur, John F., *Our Sufficiency in Christ* (Dallas: Word, 1991).

——and Wayne Mack, (eds.), *Introduction to Biblical Counseling* (Dallas: Word, 1994).

MacDonald, James, *I Really Want to Change … So, Help Me God* (Chicago: Moody Press, 2000).

Mack, Wayne, *A Homework Manual for Biblical Counseling* (Phillipsburg, NJ: P&R, 1977).

——*Your Family God's Way* (Phillipsburg, NJ: P&R, 1991).

Mahaney, C. J., *The Cross Centered Life* (Sisters, OR: Multnomah, 2002).

Powlison, David, *Seeing with New Eyes* (Phillipsburg, NJ: P&R, 2003).

——*Speaking Truth in Love: Counsel in Community* (Winston-Salem, NC: Punch Press, 2005).

Priolo, Lou, *The Heart of Anger* (Amityville, NY: Calvary Press, 1997).

——*Pleasing People* (Phillipsburg, NJ: P&R, 2007).

Sande, Ken, *The Peacemaker* (Grand Rapids, MI: Baker, 2004).

Scott, Stuart, *The Exemplary Husband* (Bemidji, MN: Focus, revised edn. 2002).

Smith, Robert D., *The Christian Counselor's Medical Desk Reference* (Stanley, NC: Timeless Texts, 2000).

Tautges, Paul. *Counseling One Another* (Wapwallopen, PA: Shepherd Press, 2016).

——*Comforting the Grieving* (Grand Rapids, MI: Zondervan, 2015).

——*Discipling the Flock* (Wapwallopen, PA: Shepherd Press, 2018).

Thomas, Curtis C., *Life in the Body of Christ* (Cape Coral, FL: Founders Press, 2006).

Tripp, Paul David. *Instruments in the Redeemer's Hands* (Phillipsburg, NJ: P&R, 2002).

——*How People Change* (Winston Salem: Punch Press, 2006).

——*War of Words* (Phillipsburg, NJ: P&R, 2000).

Welch, Edward T., *Addictions: A Banquet in the Grave* (Phillipsburg, NJ: P&R, 2001).

——*Blame It on the Brain?* (Phillipsburg, NJ: P&R, 1998).

——*When People Are Big and God Is Small* (Phillipsburg, NJ: P&R, 1997).

Whitney, Donald S., *Spiritual Disciplines for the Christian Life* (Colorado Springs, CO: NavPress, 1991).

——*Spiritual Disciplines within the Church* (Chicago: Moody Press, 1996).